THE LIFETIME SOUNDTRACK

Transcultural Music Studies

Series Editors: Simone Krüger Bridge, Liverpool John Moores University; and Britta Sweers, University of Bern

Transcultural Music Studies publishes monographs and edited collections on contemporaneous explanations surrounding the nature of music and human beings in a (post-)global world. Books in this series encompass a comprehensively wide selection of subject matters alongside a shared interest in fieldwork – physical, virtual, historical – and its complex challenges and fascinations in a postcolonial age. Topics include music's use in social, collective and psychological life; musical individuals; music in globalization and migration; music education; music, ethnicity and gender; and environmental issues.

Forthcoming

Bikutsi
A Beti Dance Music on the Rise, 1970–1990
Anja Brunner

Cultural Mapping and Musical Diversity
Edited by Britta Sweers and Sarah Ross

Provincial Headz
British Hip Hop and Critical Regionalism
Adam de Paor-Evans

THE LIFETIME SOUNDTRACK

MUSIC AND AUTOBIOGRAPHICAL MEMORY

LAUREN ISTVANDITY

SHEFFIELD UK   BRISTOL CT

Published by Equinox Publishing Ltd.

UK: Office 415, The Workstation, 15 Paternoster Row, Sheffield, South Yorkshire
S1 2BX
USA: ISD, 70 Enterprise Drive, Bristol, CT 06010

www.equinoxpub.com

First published 2019

British Library Cataloguing-in-Publication Data
A catalogue record for this book is available from the British Library.

Library of Congress Cataloging-in-Publication Data
Names: Istvandity, Lauren, author.
Title: The lifetime soundtrack : music and autobiographical memory / Lauren
   Istvandity.
Description: Bristol, CT : Equinox Publishing, 2019. | Series: Transcultural
   music studies | Includes bibliographical references and index. |
   Identifiers: LCCN 2019001543 (print) | LCCN 2019002956 (ebook) | ISBN
   9781781796306 (ePDF) | ISBN 9781781796283 (hb) | ISBN
9781781796290 (pb)
Subjects: LCSH: Music--Psychological aspects. | Memory. | Autobiography.
Classification: LCC ML3838 (ebook) | LCC ML3838 .I87 2019 (print) | DDC
   781.1/1--dc23
LC record available at https://lccn.loc.gov/2019001543

ISBN: 978 1 78179 628 3   (hardback)
        978 1 78179 629 0   (paperback)
        978 1 78179 630 6   (ePDF)

Typeset by CA Typesetting Ltd.

Contents

Acknowledgements

Warm thanks are extended to all participants in the research from which this book was written, who volunteered their memories so openly, and with such generous detail. I can only hope I have done justice to your thoughts and feelings; I feel privileged to have met you.

Thanks to my mentors Professor Sarah Baker, Dr Donna Weston and Professor Andy Bennett who guided me in establishing this research and continue to inspire me in the pursuit of music scholarship.

Thanks to fellow researchers Raphael and Kaya, for their optimism, enthusiasm and support. Thanks also to the Griffith Centre for Social and Cultural Research, and Queensland Conservatorium Research Centre.

Thanks most of all to my husband Lachlan, whose virtuous patience and kindness towards my academic work seems to know no limit.

Chapter 4 draws on concepts also contained within an article published by the author in the journal *Popular Music History* (Istvandity 2014: 136–54).

Chapter 5 draws on concepts also contained within an article published by the author in the journal *Perfect Beat* (Istvandity 2017a: 49–68).

Permissions are kindly granted by Equinox Publishing.

Introduction

> Listing the afternoon away wandering our half-acre backyard, my five-year-old self steps from tree to tree, thinking simple thoughts, exploring the dirt, grass, and embracing the golden glow of late spring. Looking up hopefully into the mulberry bush for signs of ripening handfuls of violet, ready to stain my fingers (and clothes), I catch strains of America's 'Sister Golden Hair' being rehearsed by my parents' covers band. Nearly, but not quite exasperated at having to be outside (it was just too noisy in the house), I listen for a moment. I know this one; I mumble a mistaken lyric. Unassuming, I pick my way through the prickle patches to fetch an old ice-cream container, a nice, clean one for the mulberries.

This is such a tiny speck of memory. It is barely there, and yet the quietness of the dappled afternoon, blurred vision of the mulberry bush and the seemingly endless run of my childhood backyard flood my senses when I hear this song. It is not really an important memory. It wasn't unusual for my parents to rehearse in the dining room. 'Sister Golden Hair' wasn't, and probably still isn't, my favourite song. But that's not why I'm recounting it. Here, one moment, one perspective, endowed with near palpable affect, is recreated in my mind, just in hearing the first few authoritative chords. As time goes on, the same memory is repeated, albeit obscured, the same mondegreen springs to mind ("I got so dandy-pressed" instead of "I got so damned depressed"). Although I am older and I can hear the song for what it really expresses, something entirely personal has been captured by the music. These things are paired in my mind, the memory and the music. In fact, there are many, many more memories – not just for me, but for you, and for most people – that have an inseparable connection with music.

This book presents an extended discussion on the ways in which music can become integrated into autobiographical memories. Its focus is the everyday occurrence in which a personal memory is recalled upon hearing salient music, or vice versa. It seeks to explore the depths to which human experience, and the emotion arising from this, can be encapsulated through the medium of music. Everybody interacts with music through a slightly different approach, and in turn, the way music is incorporated into personal memory can vary. There are many factors that can affect the way these two agents operate: culture, religion, access to music, and upbringing have the potential to influence and even regulate the natural relationship between music and memory. And of course, some people just don't engage with music as much as others. But insofar as music has come to be understood as an embedded part of ancient and modern societies, most people you speak with would be able to describe at least a handful of instances where music is integrated into their memory of a time, place or person. Just how this happens and why we as humans are bound to use musical memories in reflexive ways is supported in this book through the narratives of people who shared with me sometimes profound and private memories in which music plays a meaningful role. This meaning is naturally particular to them, tied closely to individual thoughts and feelings: it is autobiographical. These volunteered narratives from a group of adults in Australia portray a range of everyday acts in which music has captured the essence of lived instances, but it is precisely in the everyday where our musical memories return to surprise, overwhelm and console us. Within this book, I explore the contexts and consequences of musical remembering: while each person encounters the creation and recollection of their memories in unique ways, there are nonetheless commonalities in human experience that have helped to shape the stories conveyed here.

This book was also devised as a vehicle for theoretical and applied ideas about music and memory that, at the time of writing, have received relatively limited attention elsewhere. As discussed in Chapter 1, there is a small collection of existing academic literature that advances our thinking about how music and memory are connected, though some findings are buried within writing on contiguous areas like cultural memory and the sociology of music. In sociocultural work on musical memory, I find there is often something missing in the connections made between personal and social interactions with music. The collective adherence to music styles or subcultures that occupies this space is surely born of individual experience; inevitably, that music has become tied to events, feelings and ways of being for those individuals, and is something that will continue to constitute part of their identity. We might hear about musical memories more frequently when they are explained anecdotally – for example, talkback radio programs especially can offer listeners the opportunity to express personal reflections, "that takes me back to ...". The connection between music and memory, and by extension, nostalgia, has proven to be a lucrative method of engaging audiences across a range of mediums and platforms: "heritage rock" acts (e.g. The Rolling Stones; Paul McCartney) that seem never to cease touring (Bennett 2009); recorded or live concert video "anniversary" re-issues; tribute bands (Homan 2006); nostalgia-oriented music television and radio (e.g. "Best of the 1970s" countdown), and online programming, among other outlets, play upon the significance of music to both individuals and collectives as the basis for ongoing appeal to an ageing audience.

Despite the popularity of musical memories in everyday experience, the topic remains a niche area of analytical study. What follows here is a deep engagement with music and memory, a look at the processes that often work in the background of our minds, creating current understandings of our past and our present. There is a great deal of privilege attached to this activity of peering into someone else's life, captured in snapshots of sound. In taking advantage of souls laid bare, I have crafted something that I believe is a useful framework for thinking and talking about music that stays with us; it's called the "lifetime soundtrack". This concept provides a unique guide to the kinds of music-memory interactions raised in the forthcoming chapters. By examining in more detail the minutiae of adults' interactions with musical memories, this book provides critical insights into understanding the ways music is used to create meaning over the life course.

Autobiographical memory and the senses

Memory, in its conceptual, psychological and operational forms, is a vast area of enquiry, though for some time this was dominated by an urge to understand what it was that we as humans could remember, how long we might remember it for, and why. Along with this are investigations into memory's polar opposite – forgetting: from mental blanks, to amnesia and dementia, memory continues to be the subject of in-depth inquiry across the sciences. In the very late twentieth century, the development of new memory concepts from the humanities and social sciences called into effect the emerging field of memory studies. This umbrella term espouses a range of interdisciplinary memory research, and most often draws on core forms of cultural, social and public memory (Radstone 2008). It is here that I position my research as a new addition to these forms, such that autobiographical memory might be understood in more sociocultural terms using some of the psychological antecedents to build a strong interdisciplinary basis for a new understanding of musical memories.

At its simplest, autobiographical memory refers to memory of one's own experiences. These personal memories are usually known more technically as "episodic memories" – memories for events or sequences that involve the self, which can be differentiated from other types of memory such as procedural (how to ride a bike), and semantic (factual information), though these memories may derive from the same experiences, and may combine with episodic memory to form autobiographical memories. While sometimes the terms "episodic" and "autobiographical" are used more or less interchangeably, some schools of thought maintain these terms have alternative definitions. One of the most comprehensive arguments on the distinctions between these terms comes from psychologist Robyn Fivush. She states that autobiographical memory can be distinguished from episodic memory as a "uniquely human form of memory that moves beyond recall of experienced events to integrate perspective, interpretation, and evaluation across self, other, and time to create a personal history" (2011: 560). This suggests that autobiographical memory, while using elements of episodic memory, is a more complex system requiring self-reflection and comparison of life experiences in an introspective way over an individual's lifetime. The use of several similar terms can be confusing and, as such, for the purposes here, "autobiographical memory" is used to describe an individual's memories of their own personal experiences and knowledge for events concerning the self that occur within their lifetime.

While personal memories are part of a complex information storage system, they are highly influenced by the social and cultural contexts in which an individual finds themselves in the past and in the present. Easing away from strictly psychological descriptions of memory, there are a wide array of applications and reflections on the concept that enhance a more holistic understanding. Of particular interest here is the memory of the senses – taste, smell, hearing, vision, touch, and even affect – from a cross-disciplinary perspective. All the senses, and particularly sound, are integral to cultural histories and autobiographies alike (see Damousi and Hamilton 2017), where they add dynamic colour and shade to our memories. A range of senses besides the auditory can be seen in many of the memory narratives volunteered by participants, like this one from Matthew who spent his childhood up to the age of 14 in Indonesia:

> [Speaking of Queen's Freddie Mercury tribute concert] ... George Michael, he got up and did ... 'Somebody to Love' which is amazing, it's the best version, I reckon it's better than Freddie's version. But they use – like they get a whole gospel choir up there, a black gospel choir up there, it's just amazing. I associate that with the house we lived in called Bintaro or in an area called Bintaro [in Indonesia] ... So yeah, I always associate the floor, the Sony TV that we had ... Panasonic laser disc player, yeah and the red couches that we had which had been with us forever, I sort of associate it with that (Matthew, age 25).

Matthew sees and feels the things around him in his memory and remembers other details like the location and layout of the house. As found in many other memory narratives of sound and music in this book, the sensation of hearing here is passed over in favour of musical or contextual elements. This is in part due to the nature of story-telling – the music is not heavily described as it's assumed the listener could probably imagine the musical timbres if they didn't already know them. Moreover though, the "everyday-ness" of sound means that it can enter our consciousness without invitation, and often without a means to control it – something we are especially vulnerable to as children. So in this, as in other musical memories, a range of senses are drawn on to comprehensively reconstruct the experience when it is recalled – it is not only the sense of hearing music that is significant. This memory narrative calls attention to the ways in which senses can become entwined in memory in ways that beg for explanations beyond the psychological. It is this lack of interdisciplinary approaches to musical memory in particular that this book sets out to address.

Engaging with music

Arguably a universal concept, the notions of what constitutes music are wide-ranging. The term "music" in this research refers to a universal sense of music, resembling the description given by the Oxford Dictionary: "vocal or instrumental sounds (or both) combined in such a way as to produce beauty of form, harmony, and expression of emotion". This includes the infinite combinations of rhythm, texture, harmony and instrumentation that are part of cultural activities around the world and throughout the history of human existence. In using the word "music" and related terms such as song/piece/genre/artist/performer/composer, it was anticipated that research participants would interpret the concept to align with their own perceptions. No one genre or style of music was implied as the focus; however, due to factors such as age and cultural background, many participants referred to Western popular music, as well as music from classical and jazz genres.

The central tenet of this research relies on human interaction with music: perhaps an obvious point to make, but there are many ways in which one might engage with music, both personally and physically, which might affect the way music and memory can become associated. Certainly, a range of mediums have already been mentioned: personal music players, stereo systems and radio – in the car or at home – are all technological sources of music that find their way into autobiographical memory. A key variance to this is engagement with recorded music versus music that is played live. These two forms can create very different sorts of memories, especially in terms of the unique contexts of live music, which contrast with the ability of recorded music to be replayed. Another factor effecting musical memories is the intensity with which people listen to music, something that can change over the course of their lives; often the teen years and young adulthood are saturated with music, while middle age can see a diminished patience for new music. The degree to which our inclination to listen to music might decline over time is hard to establish, though some research indicates a narrowing of tastes over time. It is very often the music of our youth that we return to in later life, perhaps because of the personal investment in certain music (buying albums, going to concerts, connecting with friends), or perhaps because of the series of strong emotions that come with first experiences that can be associated with music from this time. With age, the way we think about music can sometimes change, just as the trends and technologies of music continue to replace what we once thought was "cool".

As mentioned, our interaction with music is not always purposeful, controlled or selected and can occur at, for example, domestic social occasions, shopping centres, sporting events, clubs, restaurants and so on. However, music that is heard incidentally, rather than intentionally, is just as likely to be remembered (or forgotten) in conjunction with everyday experiences. Instead, serendipitous encounters with music might later serve as significant points of reflection on people, places or events. A useful way of thinking about the frequency of this happening is via Anahid Kassabian's concept of "ubiquitous music" (2008, 2013), in which she suggests that a bombardment of music in everyday life has led to a developed mode of listening, one that leads us to perceive music in different ways, such that "hearing" music becomes different to "listening" to music. The ubiquity of music in modern times is contrasted in older research participants' narratives where music technologies were less available, where often interaction with music was somewhat more valued, and the memories more treasured, than in modern contexts of instantaneous musical access. Perhaps then, an increasing saturation of modern soundscapes with music is changing the way we think about music and its meaning within our lives.

One of the primary links between music and memory is identity: our engagement with music is linked to our sense of self, and we do our best to remember what it is that makes us who we are by reflecting on moments that are important to us. Music sociologist Simon Frith makes this connection when he says:

> The experience of pop music is an experience of identity: in responding to a song, we are drawn, haphazardly, into emotional alliances with the performers and with the performers' other fans. Because of its qualities of abstractness, music is, by nature, an individualizing form. We absorb songs into our own lives and rhythm into our own bodies; they have a looseness of reference that makes them immediately accessible. At the same time, and equally significantly, music is obviously collective. We hear things as music because their sounds obey a more or less familiar cultural logic, and for most music listeners (who are not themselves music makers) this logic is out of our control (Frith 1996: 121).

Though Frith is referring to popular music here, the same could be said of any music with which one is most familiar, and to which one most easily takes. Frith raises a significant point about the processes of individualization, where interpretation of musical elements and combinations leads us to embody music as our own, despite its place within collective culture, something that is expanded upon in Chapter 2. As we accumulate musical memories over time, there is a need to release some of those which hold less importance in comparison to others. This process of *memory canonization* is something I assert is part of this individualization process and helps to form the "lifetime soundtrack".

The lifetime soundtrack: A framework

As an original way of conceptualizing musical memories, I have devised the idea of the lifetime soundtrack, which I define as a metaphorical collection of music that relates in unique and personal ways to a person's autobiographical memories. Drawing on notions of memory and the senses, the lifetime soundtrack reflects Pillemer's (1998) suggestion that autobiographical memory can be thought of as a primarily visual reconstruction comparable to film reel. Parallels can also be drawn between the soundtrack to a film and music that accompanies personal memories. The lifetime soundtrack is limited to music that one has experienced personally; however this music is often experienced in social and cultural contexts that effect the way it might become associated with memory. Music within the soundtrack is not bound to correspond with an individual's music taste, as we experience a range of music in daily life outside of this, though changes in listening habits may become evident in the lifetime soundtrack over time. Likewise, the lifetime soundtrack is not typically comprised of music and memories that engender one particular emotion (e.g. happiness); it encompasses music that reminds one of a range of personal experiences, potentially provoking both pleasant and unpleasant emotions. In this way, one's soundtrack is *not* a "greatest hits" collection, though in moments of reflection it could be used for this purpose. Rather, the lifetime soundtrack is a personal aural record of life, a stream that somewhat equitably collects musical memories with the passing of time.

As mentioned, anecdotal description and colloquial analysis of musical memories is rather common; despite this, there is no existing academic framework that can effectively explain this relationship, or facilitate in-depth examination. The concept of the lifetime soundtrack is the first of its kind, finding an unclaimed niche between the associated field of music sociology and the intricacies of autobiographical memory. It is necessarily both inclusive and exclusive, due to the diverse nature of interrelated topics: the lifetime soundtrack intersects a range of subfields and topic areas including emotion (affect), taste, youth, ageing, consumption, technology, musicianship, and beyond. Current research in music sociology looks to broader, and often more collective, trends in the connection between identity and music consumption, place, youth and ageing, scenes, ethnicity, gender and meaning-making amongst other things, for example, works by Simon Frith, Tia DeNora, Andy Bennett, David Hesmondhalgh, Sara Cohen, and others. However, the remit of music sociology generally does not usually seek to understand the relationship between individuals and music on a micro-level, and often passes over memory as an element within social processes. Similarly, autobiographical memory has been predominantly studied within the sciences for what it can tell us about the mind through quantitative, large-scale research projects, where there is a clear gap for focused, smaller-scale qualitative research. As the next chapter explains in more detail, the innovation of the lifetime soundtrack lies in its integration of both memory studies and music sociology in a way that is widely applicable across disciplines, finally providing a framework and defined terms through which to discuss a curiosity of everyday life that has been obscured within broader research for decades.

In the following chapters, the finer details and possibilities of the soundtrack are explored, both theoretically and through direct reference to real-life memory narratives gathered from research participants. The rationale for the nomenclature of a "lifetime" soundtrack is based on two interrelated concepts that will be extrapolated in the coming pages. The first is the direct reference the lifetime soundtrack can make in temporal terms to one's life: musical referents can correspond to anything from a precise moment to a number of years that can be characterized by a set of circumstances. The lifetime soundtrack's relation to time and space is one of the fundamental components that make individual soundtracks distinct, even when musical content between two soundtracks is similar. The second is the development of the soundtrack over time, and the changing relationship that might develop with the soundtrack through changing life circumstances, the addition of new material and reflexive listening practices. When new musical memories are formed, and we mature in our thoughts and feelings, older parts of the lifetime soundtrack might be re-evaluated. This is a constant process which I alluded to earlier as one of canonization, which reflects the similarity between the development of personal soundtracks and the ways in which the prevailing histories of music genres are formed (see Kärjä 2006).

While the lifetime soundtrack provides the framework to be eked out through reflection on memory narratives, the basis for the theoretical development of both music and memory in this book draws on both sociocultural and psychological theories. The justification for doing this is simple: the formation of and reflection upon musical memories cannot easily be explained through exclusive use of either social or scientific theories – doing so gives an incomplete picture. Rather, this research encourages an interdisciplinary approach to autobiographical memory that meets with thorough appreciation of how music affects the brain, but also how musical affects and activities are socially constructed.

Methods

The autobiographical stories of 28 people were explored in the research that underlies this book. Narratives were collected from individuals during one-on-one interviews that were semi-structured, designed to elicit musical memories through focused discussion of participants' life stories. Questions guided interview participants to describe those experiences which were often brought to mind upon hearing certain music, and the context in which they occurred. Thematic prompts relating to time and circumstance were used to this effect, for example, "what kind of music was around at home when you were growing up?", or "is there particular music that reminds you of major events in your life?" The mode of listening – recorded or live music, and the technology used – was accounted for but not necessarily prompted so as to produce as wide a range of responses as possible. This sort of questioning allowed for a conversational interaction between researcher and participant where participants could freely add contextual information to their narratives. With the consent of participants, our interviews were recorded, and the transcripts were thematically coded and analysed. The use of music within interviews was considered in relation to the potential effects on interview outcomes – certainly, playing music selected by participants might encourage more detailed memories than using imagination alone, however this could place some people at a disadvantage should they not have access to music that forms a significant part of their lifetime soundtrack. As a result, audible music was absent for most interviews; instead the structure drew upon on a "life story" approach (Atkinson 1998; McAdams 2001). One interviewee did use music during their interview, because – aptly – he had recently compiled a playlist for his sixtieth birthday. The playlist consisted of music that was associated with early childhood through to the present, the only shortcoming being that it didn't contain music with which the participant might have had negative associations – though this information was still gathered verbally in the absence of music.

The interviewees gathered for this research were aged from 18 to 82 years of various cultural backgrounds, residing in south-east Queensland at the time of interview. Queensland is the second largest state in Australia, with metropolitan centres dotting the east coast, and large areas of farmland and mining communities positioned in the western interior. Residents of south-east Queensland generally inhabit metro areas: all of the participants in this research lived in the state's larger cities of Brisbane and the Gold Coast. The majority of participants were of an Anglo-European background, with the family origin of three participants in south-east Asia. In a way that is not un-representative of Australia's multiculturalism, of the 28 participants 20 were born in Australia, three in New Zealand, three in the United Kingdom, one in Indonesia, and one in Canada; most people noted these places were also the location of their childhood. Two family groups (three and four members each) took part in interviews, which allowed for some comparison between older and younger people with shared experiences. The majority of interviewees were from a range of middle- and working-class backgrounds; however, discussions of class were not entered into during interviews. Certainly, Australians experience contrasting economic positions found in many Western nations; despite this, class in Australia is not always easily identifiable due to mismatches between wealth and other class markers such as education, income, and political alignment (Kelley and McAllister 1985). As such, class does not feature as an aspect of analysis in this book, yet could serve as a worthy point of further investigation in terms of how the lifetime soundtrack interacts with existing theories of music and class within sociology. Another point worth mentioning about the research participants is the ratio of musicians to non-musicians in the cohort: 16 people described themselves as non-musicians, while 12 participants noted their involvement with music on an amateur or professional level. To protect the identity of participants, the use of pseudonyms has been employed throughout this book. Qualitative analysis of interviews revealed several leading themes: tales of people, places and eras were accompanied by a periphery of common intersections – childhood, emotion, connection to musical elements, identity, and musicianship. In what follows, these ideas and many beyond are explored and critiqued for their occurrence in the everyday, and their reflexive use as a tool for meaning-making over a lifetime.

Organization of the book

The first chapter has two principal objectives: first, it will provide the reader with a thorough overview of the functions of autobiographical memory and music by outlining current perspectives of musical memory in sociocultural literature. The second function of this chapter is to explore theoretical concepts that are central to the rest of the book, including ideas pertaining to the lifetime soundtrack, including the ways in which musical memory is created and re-created in everyday life. This chapter also points to the gaps in how musical memories are discussed, creating a rationale for future use of the lifetime soundtrack in music and memory research.

Chapter 2 is devoted to the beginnings of the lifetime soundtrack in childhood, and the early stages of its development through adolescence and young adulthood. The development of the soundtrack is shown to be socially constructed in childhood, where family members play a critical role in mediating music experience. The chapter focuses on the home as the place of music interaction – whether as recorded music or family music-making, heard in shared living areas or private bedroom spaces. Participants' narratives also reveal the degree to which caregivers' attitudes towards, and value of, music can alter the relationship they have with music throughout their life. The aforementioned process of canonization is here explained: as more musical memories are accrued, we often make unconscious decisions to unhinge some of these instances from our soundtrack, making the lifetime soundtrack both dynamic and responsive.

The influence of musical affect and emotional investment is the topic of Chapter 3. It first looks to the psychological connections between music and emotion, where a triangulation between music, emotion and memory becomes apparent. Complex relationships with music and affect are demonstrated in memory narratives, which include sometimes unexpected physical and mental responses to listening. Therein, both commonplace and novel scenarios for the inception of emotional memories are unpacked, including romantic relationships, bereavement and loss, and lifetime milestones. The chapter also raises questions about the purposeful use of music to provoke emotion, and the intention behind, and effect of, the creation of literal soundtracks for special events.

The fourth chapter in this book conceptualizes the link between music and autobiographical memory through reference to philosophical ideas of the archive. I propose that elements pertaining to music listening experience are able to effectively capture and store personal memories, which can then be retrieved upon rehearing salient music, where music acts as a personal *lieux de memoire*. To support this theory, I compare the fidelity of music technology and the fallibility of human memory. The chapter argues that musical elements such as lyrics and sound, as well as the para-musical elements of listening technology and physical entrainment, produce an effective archival system for autobiographical experiences due to the complementary properties of music and memory. This chapter is supported by the particularly unique ways participants described their connection with music; the typically ineffable nature of music perception is emphasized here through the range of ways interviewees perceived their relationship between sounds, lyrics, movement and technology.

Chapter 5 concentrates on the experience of research participants who identified as being musically trained – be that in a professional or amateur practice. Musical memories narrated by people who participated in music-making possessed characteristics that were distinct in a number of ways. Concepts such as emotion, identity and embodiment are covered in this chapter with special emphasis on how these aspects are enacted for musicians in both performative and listening contexts. The chapter also draws on musicians' experience of music-making as "work", which can result in more negative emotional associations with music than provided by non-musicians. It offers suggestions as to why and how musicians might experience music differently, potentially enacting different practices of memorialization.

Chapter 6 seeks out the meaning and use of the lifetime soundtrack, expounding on themes of previous chapters. Looking to the experiences of both older and younger participants' reflection on their soundtrack, the chapter is particularly concerned with the effects of internal and external change on the lifetime soundtrack. Ageing is one of the major factors that can cause change in daily life: this chapter sees ageing as a process that can modulate attitudes, bodies, musicality and the relationship we have with music as it looks more closely at peak times of music use: adolescence and post-retirement. The progression of time also increases the likelihood that musical trends – that is, production and consumption – will change. I also consider in more detail the capitalization of music markets upon ageing consumer cultures, and how the repetition of music from the baby-boomer era helps to consolidate the soundtracks of that generation.

The final concluding chapter synthesizes ideas raised by the previous chapters to produce a sociocultural perspective on the workings of musical autobiographical memories in everyday life. Seven key characteristics of the lifetime soundtrack are summarized for their relation to a renewed perspective on memory, and the soundtrack is discussed in terms of future applications in memory and music research. Here I argue for a greater consideration of autobiographical memory within music sociology and cultural studies research, such that memory can be seen as a missing intermediary link in studies of music perception and social interaction. Finally, the chapter emphasizes the importance of musical memories as a tool for meaning-making throughout life, but especially in older individuals. Ways in which this concept may be used in wider contexts are discussed with reference to areas both within and beyond memory studies. This book provides a new perspective on the ways in which music and memory are simultaneously enacted and how instances of their interaction are used and re-used to instil a sense of meaning throughout the life course, where the ever-increasing presence of music in everyday life offers countless opportunities for the intermingling of music and memory.

1 Assembling an Interdisciplinary Approach to Musical Memories

> [At mass] I used to sit up – because [my] hearing's going a bit – so I sat up close to the pulpit so I could hear what was going on, and I tend to sing quite lustily, because I like to exercise my lungs. If you're not going to sing properly..! And as the hymns would come and go, I'd sing, and this little blighter [the minister] was up there "who's that singing? I've got you!" And then on the way out, the processional song, so I'd be singing away and he'd be coming up the aisle and he'd say "gotcha". Next thing I know … he wants to form a singing group to perform at the nine o'clock mass and he wants all males … they called us The Three Tenors! We weren't particularly tenors … but we got up there and sang and it got to the stage where every time I think of Father Quirk I think of that choir, every time I think of that choir, I think of the organist, every time I think of the organist I think of us singing hymns (Vincent, age 77).

The act of music triggering reminiscence, such as in Vincent's story above, is commonplace; however, its novelty – that music associates with memory in unexpected ways – means that it has retained the interest of scholars and the public over time. In anecdotal descriptions of musical memories retold through modern media, there is a recurring theme of wonderment and enjoyment. What this suggests, though, is the desire for greater understanding of how and why music can mean so much in our memories – the invocation of significant personal memories through the texture of a guitar lick or the aptness of a lyric's phrase presents itself as a curious souvenir of the past, sometimes retrieved and re-retrieved with repeat fascination at their connection. Though this research does not propose to resolve completely the ins and outs of the association between music and memory, it does take steps to create a framework and model for understanding the assemblage of music into a canon related to our life experiences, that is, the lifetime soundtrack.

There is much discussion and deliberation on the formation, manifestation and, less often, the meaning of musical memories that can be found in scholarly study of memory, and of music. This chapter brings together some of the most pertinent concepts underscoring the integration of these two agents; however, working through this does require some flexibility in terms of traditional academic boundaries, and open-mindedness from the reader. As noted in the introductory chapter, this book handles autobiographical memory in a particular way: there is a distinct sociological disposition in much of the discussion henceforth, because an understanding of the meaning and use of the lifetime soundtrack, contextually situated, is the primary aim of the research. This is often interrupted by the overtly psychological approach to autobiographical memory taken in much published research, contrasting with the ease with which concepts of collective memory intercept sociocultural theories. In considering how autobiographical memory might interact with memory for music and vice versa, it is almost impossible to separate or entirely ignore the fascinating psychological concepts which underpin personal memory. In fact, some of these concepts prove very useful in formulating theoretical frameworks regarding musically motivated autobiographical memory, and so there is a rationalized need for an appreciation, or even a re-appraisal, of how memory is treated within and beyond one's own discipline.

This chapter provides an overview of the progress of music and memory research across fields including cultural studies, sociology and psychology. In doing so it demonstrates the widespread nature of existing knowledge and underscores the need for frameworks such as the lifetime soundtrack in helping to make sense of what we know about music and memory. It outlines the overlapping functions of both memory and music and underscores the context of everyday life in which these functions play out. This chapter will also explore the location of the lifetime soundtrack between the individual and the collective.

Memory functions, narrative, and the life story

The grand scale of a "lifetime" is used in this research to allow for the broad study of musical memories as networks that are constantly in flux. Certainly, as memories accumulate there is a need to both remember and forget – especially that which no longer serves us. In this research, older and younger people were interviewed, all with varied and interesting opinions on what their lifetime soundtrack looked like in that moment, providing coverage of the lifetime soundtrack at different times in life. A significant reason for the use of this temporal boundary relates to the stories or narratives that we develop about ourselves and our experiences over the duration of a lifetime. Using a narrative approach grounded in psychology, McAdams (2005, 2008) proposes that individuals adopt the medium of stories to understanding meaning within their lives:

> ... the stories we construct to make sense of our lives are funda-
> mentally about our struggle to reconcile who we imagine we were,
> are, and might be in our heads and bodies with who we were,
> are and might be in the social contexts of family, community, the
> workplace, ethnicity, religion, gender, social class, and culture writ
> large. *The self comes to terms with society through narrative iden-*
> *tity* (2008: 242–43, emphasis original).

Collectively, these stories form an overarching "life story", which changes
with the addition of new or repeated experiences. The life story essentially
sits alongside the lifetime soundtrack and is a useful concept for understanding how narratives involving music might be positioned within greater discourses of narrative identity. The concept of narrative itself has been applied
in a range of disciplines, not least of all in memory studies. Schank and Abelson (1995: 44) contend that stories are the basis of our understanding, and
that in order to remember our experiences we must recall and retell stories
of them. According to them, "telling stories is fundamentally a memory reinforcing process. The more you tell, the more you remember". Stories selected
as significant aspects of experience tend to portray an individual's identity,
cultural values and general attitudes. They are used not only introspectively
but as a medium to communicate with others. McAdams notes that the life
story is a function of autobiographical memory rather than a replication of
it – a life story does not contain all remembered aspects of experience; rather
it "consists of a more delimited set of temporally and thematically organised
scenes and scripts that together constitute identity" (McAdams 2001: 117).

Linked to ideas of the life story are the everyday social functions of autobiographical memory. It has been widely acknowledged that memory for personal experience serves three principal functions: self, social and directive
(Cohen 1996; Alea and Bluck 2003; Bluck 2003; Fivush 2011; Williams,
Conway and Cohen 2008). Memory directives are remembered events that
can have an enduring influence that extends beyond the immediate circumstance (Pillemer 1998: 65); situations in which we use memory directives are
those where we rely on our past experiences to guide our actions or those of
others. The social function of autobiographical memory relates the individual to the collective by helping us maintain relationships, pass on knowledge,
and show or elicit empathy with others (Alea and Bluck 2003). The third,
and in the current context, most important function of memory regards the
perpetuation of the self and the regulation of current and past identities. All
three functions often manifest by way of stories, whether these are relayed to
others or rehearsed internally. These stories usually relate to events that one
has personally experienced, that is, autobiographical memory, and help to
make up who we are. Identity is therefore closely tied to memory, and connection with these aspects can be evidenced in cultural choices, especially music

(Frith 1981; North and Hargreaves 1999; DeNora 2000; Rentfrow and Gosling 2003). The stories we tell using music can be verbal recollections of what that music signifies but could also be communicated in broad ways through sharing of the music itself. This aspect is part of the reason music is a particularly dynamic medium through which memory can be enacted.

The functions of music

While the need for memory in everyday life has a rational and explainable basis, our apparent need for music and its function in personal and social contexts has been a topic of much debate amongst anthropologists, scientists and philosophers alike. There is much evidence to propose that music has existed as long as humans themselves, evolving around the same time as language; however, there are few clear reasons for this development. It has been argued that music doesn't seem to serve as an essential survival mechanism – that is, life without music would carry on very much as before. However, there are some convincing reasons for the function of music that could in fact aid the survival of the species, finding a basis in communication, and the fulfilment of social and emotional needs. Anthropological reasoning for the existence of music often refers to uses such as social bonding and emotional cohesion (e.g. celebration, or hunting), coordination of group hunting, and sexual differentiation among males (see Huron 2001; Mithen 2006; Thompson 2015). Throughout different cultures and time periods, humans have continued to use music for increasingly sophisticated forms of these original functions or uses of music. In modern psychology and sociology, there is a greater focus on the function of music for individuals within societal contexts, which aligns with the development of postmodern identity theory based on reflexivity (e.g. Giddens 1991), and, among other things, the advent of popular music, youth cultures, and personalized listening. Merriam's (1964) anthropological identification of ten functions of music became the foundation for research into the cognitive and emotional functions of music in the field of psychology. These include emotional expression, aesthetic enjoyment, entertainment, communication, symbolic representation, physical response, conformity, ritual, continuity of culture, and integration of society. Hargreaves and North (1999) argue that all of Merriam's psychological functions of music can be related to social contexts or uses, and advocate for a more straightforward typology of music's functions to the management of mood (emotion), self-identity and interpersonal relationships. These ideas are evidenced across the psychology and sociology of music – highlighting the complexity of musical memories and the need for interdisciplinary approaches to the topic.

The perceived function of music to alter or manage moods and behaviour has received a great deal of attention in the psychology behind music and emotion. Music has been shown to both enhance emotion (e.g. listening to sad music when sad; Van den Tol and Edwards 2013) and subvert moods or action (e.g. music in shopping malls, Eroglu *et al.* 2005; or in dementia therapies, McDermott *et al.* 2013) for the purposes of well-being. The connections between emotion and music are often emphasized in adolescence, a time in which young people often invest – socially, emotionally, financially and personally – in music, and the consumption of music in youth can be particularly useful for reflection on change and new experiences (e.g. Saarikallio and Erkkilä 2007). DeNora (2000: 53) uses the term "emotion work" to describe the reflexive use of music "as a resource for modulating and structuring the parameters of aesthetic agency", which can in turn help to consolidate a sense of self. DeNora's approach is a sociological one, and it is through this lens that much work has been done to make connections between music, emotion and personal identity. Often described as a "badge" of individual identity (Frith 1981: 258), developing personal taste, sharing music and taking part in musical subcultures are all activities that help us to formulate parts of our identity, and to display this to others; however Hesmondhalgh (2008) warns this may not always be as positive a process as most commonly thought due to the increasing politicization of music taste and the opportunity for negative experiences.

When Hargreaves and North refer to the function of music for the management of relationships, they imply here a range of interpersonal relationships, some of which hark back to the original uses of music by early humans. Frith (1981) explains that our personal musical identity is also used to communicate with others, to help sort out where we fit in the collective. Further, listening to or making music facilitates social bonds and aids a sense of belonging with others (Rentfrow and Gosling 2006). The use of music for communication differs between cultures – the study of which forms the basis for much research in the area of ethnomusicology. The functions of memory and music overlap in interesting ways that are instructive in regard to their integration in everyday life. Both are used as a way of facilitating social relationships, of communicating with others, and both are important to the development and consolidation of personal identity. While music lacks the directive function of memory, it can become a significant tool for the management of daily affect. Though this research is less concerned with the functional aspects of music and memory, it still looks to forge a greater understanding of their relationship in terms of their function in social and private life.

Acts and practices of remembering

With memory and music now established as necessary components of everyday activity, I turn to accounting for some of the ways in which memory is actually enacted, and how this can be related to music. One of the most significant traits of autobiographical memory recall is that it comprises an ongoing reconstruction of past encounters, rather than a faithful replication of an individual's experience. Autobiographical memory does not act as a compendium for everything that ever happened to an individual; memory should be thought of as a process, rather than a *thing* (Brockmeier 2010). Schacter explains the nature of autobiographical memory as malleable and open to influence:

> We do not record our experiences the way a camera records them ... we extract key elements from our experiences and store them. We then recreate or reconstruct our experiences rather than retrieve copies of them. Sometimes, in the process of reconstructing we add on feelings, beliefs, or even knowledge we obtained after the experience (2001: 9).

Schacter's account of memory implies that facets of experience from different chronologies are pulled together and re-evaluated in the present moment. This process requires what is commonly referred to in the literature as memory "rehearsal", which is the activity of reminiscing intentionally, usually in order to retell an autobiographical story in social contexts. It is at the point of recounting a story that the reconstruction of the memory using selective details takes place. Each element of an experience that is recorded in memory can be redesigned, exaggerated or omitted by the individual in accordance with the social situation, which can impact the way in which the event is subsequently remembered and re-told by the narrator (Skowronski and Walker 2004). At the same time as we describe the processes of remembering, we are also forgetting, purposefully and unintentionally, details which might no longer be useful to us in everyday life. What is curious, then, is the persistence of music in memory: while on the surface, music might seem one of the less important aspects of experience that one might need to recall throughout life, I argue that one of the significant roles music plays is to continually juxtapose us with our past selves, and to provide a means through which we can create personal meaning over the course of a life. To this end, the lifetime soundtrack acts as a framework in which reflexive activities can take place. In what follows, I outline the ways in which musical memories come to be created, and the integration of memory with music as guided by what is currently known about the processes of memory.

Autobiographical memories can be recalled in two ways – voluntarily and involuntarily. An involuntary autobiographical memory is a "memory of a personal experience brought to consciousness with apparent spontaneity, that is, without preceding attempts at retrieving it" (Berntsen 1996: 435), also termed "passive remembering" (Spence 1988). Conversely, voluntary memories are personal memories that "follow a controlled, strategic retrieval process" (Rubin and Berntsen 2009: 679). Memories that are associated with or are triggered by music can be both voluntarily and involuntarily recalled or prompted. According to Ben Anderson, a voluntary *musical* memory involves "the deliberate use of music to recollect, reminisce or recreate the content or mood of an already defined memory" (2004: 13). By way of contrast, involuntary musical memories are those that are unbidden but are triggered by the presence of music that has not been deliberately chosen by the listener. Perhaps too, the context of the original intersection between music and a potential memory subject was also beyond the control of the listener. This could be thought of as "passive listening" – many examples of which occur in childhood where in most instances the music is mediated by adults in authority, such as in the home (see Chapter 2) or at times when the individual is not fully engaged with, but aware of, music that is present in their environment. Such associations are only realized when the memory is subsequently brought to mind through hearing integrated music sometime after the original occurrence. This could happen, for example, when listening to the radio or hearing music in public spaces such as shopping centres, waiting rooms, cafés and bars. Via these "practices of remembering", musical memories are strengthened through embodiment in everyday activities (Anderson 2004).

Nostalgia

The concept of nostalgia is problematic, yet important to acknowledge in laying out the range of ways in which music and memory intersect, especially in retrospective memory practices. Modern definitions of nostalgia imply a range of emotional conditions of memory, from "the state of being homesick" to "a wistful or excessively sentimental yearning for return to, or of, some past period or irrecoverable condition" (Merriam Webster Dictionary 2018). This implies nostalgia is an affect associated with memory or the act of recollection, though scholars point to it as one that is a "contested and culturally loaded concept often equated with simulated forms of sentimentality" (Bull 2009: 91). There is some debate over whether nostalgia can be characterized as a positive or negative affect (or some combination of the two). Ross (1992) suggests that despite its origin in sadness (stemming from a longing for person or place), modern nostalgia more often refers to a positive experience of reflecting on the past. Scherer and colleagues (2001) describe nostalgia as one of the core emotions produced when listening to music: what is significant is the consideration here of nostalgia as an emotion, rather than a form of memory.

Reflecting on musical memory, like any memory, has the potential to evoke feelings of nostalgia for both the narrator of the experience, and those listening – sometimes resulting in a mediated sense of nostalgia that can also manifest in the appeal of contemporary versions of "retro" culture (see Hogarty 2016; van der Hoeven 2014). As the chapters of this book explain, music can come to represent strong feelings and trigger a range of sensations that may be reflected on with a sense of nostalgia, something that has found its way into psychological research on musical memories (e.g. Barrett *et al.* 2010; Michels-Ratliff and Ennis 2016). In describing the exploitation of nostalgia in commodification and advertising, Bull argues that the experience of the individual goes beyond "fabricated constructions of the culture industry" (2009: 91), permitting unique interactions with nostalgia on an everyday level. Also coming to the defence of nostalgia in thinking about musical memory is the extensive scholarship penned by Emily Keightley and Michael Pickering (Pickering and Keightley 2006, 2015; Keightley and Pickering 2012). The authors call for the reframing of nostalgia from its negative connotations, describing it as a driving force behind modern movements of auto/biography, local history and folklore, where such interests "signal a collective desire to reconnect with what has apparently been lost, or reassess what has apparently been gained" (Keightley and Pickering 2012: 114).

Though nostalgia can be active as a form of musical reminiscence, it is difficult to ascertain the degree to which it might influence the memory narratives collected for this research. As noted, it is potentially inherent in any reflective practice that produces feelings of "wistful sentimentality". People in my research rarely referred directly to nostalgia to describe what they were feeling when speaking about their memories. One exception was Will, who said:

> I always remember, like Sundays for me are synonymous with Beethoven or Tchaikovsky or Bach, maybe some Grieg ... just on a Sunday, my Dad reading the paper. That's from an early age, every single Sunday there was classical music on, early morning. And sit and read the paper so, definitely in my new house, yeah since I was ten. Don't necessarily remember that beforehand, but from ten, the nice room of the house, that sort of Sunday, you go in there, especially in summer. So ... now because of it, like today – no one was in the house and I feel that it's a Sunday, even though it's a public holiday Monday, I will put on classical music, because I don't know, it's a nostalgia thing or whatever (Will, age 26).

In this instance, nostalgic feelings prompt Will to engage with distinct listening practices, the same kind of association that might lead one to seek out other sensations brought on by activities such as smoking, drinking or eating to further immerse themselves in a past time and place. Interview questions were not designed with the evocation of nostalgia in mind; however, this doesn't mean participants may not have interpreted my questions as such. Admittedly, the theories I have applied here tend to skirt the idea of nostalgia, though this outcome was not necessarily intentional. Rather, in exploring the narratives provided by participants, I have tried to avoid applying too many preconceived ideas about how and why people might be thinking about music in certain ways. At the same time, it is very possible that nostalgic reflection was at play while stories were being relayed, which suggests a particular level of emotional engagement between participants and their lifetime soundtrack.

Manifestations of musical memories

Memories often include sensations that were present in the original circumstances; besides music and sound, this can include smell, taste, and visual elements. The latter element in particular is widely acknowledged as one of the primary ways we relive memories – often playing back through visual representations. Some psychologists note the experience of vivid or "flashbulb memories" as being highly visual (Pillemer 1998; Conway 2009). By definition, flashbulb memories are those that starkly recall the circumstances in which one learned of a surprising or consequential event (Brown and Kulik 1977: 73), usually one with wide societal impacts. The high level of detail in these memories can sometimes be proved erroneous due to the effects of trauma or stress. Vivid memories, on the other hand, describe autobiographical memories that are sharply defined in recollection (Rubin and Kozin 1984), but relate more to personal, rather than widely shared, events. Though discussions of these concepts emphasize visual elements, less is known about the way music is incorporated into vivid memories. One exception is the research conducted by Gabrielsson (2011), who in seeking to find out more about strong experiences with music, gathered over 1300 (primarily) written descriptions from 1000 participants. Accounts were analysed to reveal at least 150 different reactions to strong experiences with music, with topics ranging through major events (e.g. weddings and funerals), temporal periods (e.g. childhood, teenage years), physical reactions, perception (e.g. auditory, visual, tactile, etc.), cognition (e.g. changed attitude, loss of control), emotions, and transcendental states. Importantly, Gabrielsson does not discuss these interactions in terms of memory; however the narratives provided are intrinsically borne of memory and music interaction.

Below is an example of a flashbulb memory associated with music, described by an interviewee in my study, Vincent:

> The first music I ever remember was on V.E. Day in 1945, in August,[1] when the Japanese surrendered and I was in Nambour [Queensland]. It was holidays, I walked up the street and down the street – now you have to remember … from the mid-30s til the mid-40s the only source of any music generally speaking was the ABC,[2] on a wireless if you happened to have a wireless, and not everybody

had a wireless ... so we didn't have a lot of music. But walking up the street, every shopfront doorway I went to, there were the young women who worked in there, and they were all singing the same song, and this really impressed me, and the same song was in my mind when I started talking and now it's faded out for a second. They'd linked arms and they were waltzing back and forth, waltzing back and forth kicking their legs up and doing everything else ... but every time I heard that song I was immediately back on V.E. Day, walking out Currie Street, Nambour (Vincent, age 77).

Later in the interview it is revealed the song was 'The Hokey Pokey'.[3] Vincent's memory describes his experience of celebrations in his home town upon the declaration of the end of World War Two. Certainly, celebrations like those described would have occurred in many different places and been experienced by many different people. Although each individual may have a different recollection of what occurred at that particular time, it is the notion that many people can relate a memory to the same day in history that makes this a musical flashbulb memory. These sorts of memories are sometimes related to collective experiences, where music, cultures and events taking place are relevant to many people. For example, autobiographical memories of the Woodstock festival, or thinking about your circumstances when you first heard of the death of a music icon (e.g. John Lennon, David Bowie) might be the source of flashbulb memories for a great number of people.

Many narratives described in this book are vividly recalled but are more autobiographical and singularly meaningful in their contexts. An impressive example comes from Paul:

I've got very vivid memories of the first time I heard [Billy Bragg's] music, and it's a particular song called 'The Saturday Boy' ... he sings in a sort of a deep, south London accent, ... even though he's quite a skilled musician he comes from a punk aesthetic so he was playing quite rough guitar, he was singing 'The Saturday Boy', [it] is basically an unrequited love song and in the middle of it there's a gorgeous trumpet or flugal horn solo, so there's this beautiful contrast between this real roughness of the guitar playing, the kind of almost clumsy song lyrics and then this quite sublime trumpet solo in the middle of the piece ... And um, I must have been 15 or 16 and after a night of drinking at a friend's place, drinking cask wine and that kind of thing. He had an older brother who came home and who had just been to a sex worker. And so I was having a good time kind of drinking with my friend ... and then his brother came home and he was a bit of a cave man and he was describing to us what he'd done with this sex worker ... and I remember feeling deeply uncomfortable in this situation thinking "oh I'm a long way from home and I really just want to go home. It doesn't seem quite right, this seems quite rough to me, like I don't really belong here" and anyway um then, that song was put on and I don't think it was communally put on ... it just happened to be on in the background and that trumpet solo came and I thought, well – I was very moved by the music at that time. It seemed quite sublime even in its roughness, so there's something about the very particular situation, I could draw the room we were in actually if necessary like a map of it anyway, and, yeah ... from that moment I felt well, beauty can come from the most awful ugly places, that it's possible to connect with your friends very deeply over music (Paul, age 42).

This description from Paul incorporates both visual and aural aspects that contribute to the intensity of the memory. The narrator can recall in great detail the layout of the house, and the scenario in which he found himself. This is paired with an eloquent appraisal of the music – perhaps something that he has come to understand since this event. The musical analogy seems to dually serve as a description of Paul's physical surroundings, further embedding the visual details of the situation into memory. In the meantime, this recollection has served as a lesson to Paul, both about music and the nature of life itself.

In presenting the varying ways in which music can trigger memory, an underlying concept about the link between autobiographical memory and music can be broached. The acknowledgement by scholars that sensory information, especially a visual aspect, is usually incorporated into memory suggests that music would form part of the recollected aural environment at the time of the experience. Unlike other atmospheric sounds that might also be included in memory, such as traffic noise, the singing of birds, or the chatter in a café, music as an aural aspect of memory can be reproduced, for the most part, to sound as it did at the time of encoding. Therefore, rather than fulfilling a role purely as a background sound, music creates a strong connection between aural and visual elements of memory, with the re-hearing of music triggering often visual elements of experience. Music can also embody something more personal than these other sounds, due to its complexity and ability to affect emotions in strong and sometimes unexpected ways.

While the rich traces of memory reveal the power of the mind to re-generate past events in detail, not all memories need to be vivid in order to be remembered, or to be personally meaningful. In another act of remembering, "generic memory" can be used reflexively to effectively abbreviate the past. This term is defined by Groves and colleagues to describe an accumulation of similar experiences over time, where events tend to blur together (2004: 216). This term is somewhat problematic because it implies that such memories are inconsequential or of little significance. As an alternative, I here implement the term "cloud memories" to describe these recollections when speaking with interviewees. As a concept that deviates slightly from generic memory, I define a cloud memory as a representation of a collection of experiences over a self-imposed temporal period and typically comprises repeated experiences within physical places and locations. These are often bound by individual circumstances, for example "when I was pregnant with my first child" or "after I left school but before I began working". Cloud memories can also be characterized by an atmosphere or affect that is perceived by the individual as representative of the time period collectively. Participants often recalled music genres or albums that reminded them of these temporal periods, rather than associating individual songs. The following excerpt from Jeremy's interview is a good example of a cloud memory:

> Yeah there's 'Strung Out', *Suburban Teenage Wasteland Blues*. It wouldn't have been when I first listened to it, but they're probably one of my favourite punk rock bands ever, and for some reason, that album reminds me of when I lived in Calgary [Canada], and, yeah I don't know why, I think I listened to that and then I think their new album came out when I was living there and that was awesome. I remember putting it on a lot when I was going to sleep (Jeremy, age 36).

In Jeremy's description, it is interesting to note the sense of time that is implied. He says this album characterizes a certain period of his life that is also aligned with his geographic location at the time. The music is already familiar to him, which enables it to be used more flexibly within memory over time. Further, the music's integration with a repeated activity (sleeping) enhances the association between the music and a certain temporal period. The temporal references suggest this memory is spread out over time, and therefore constitutes a cloud memory. Memory narratives that appear in this book vary in the depth of detail provided. Some have less detail than Jeremy's cloud memory above, and others differ in description level through to the extremely vivid. The significance of flashbulb, vivid, or more collectively assembled memory against each other is contestable – the value of an individual's memories is nearly always dependent on the circumstances in which they were formed and are further subject to the context of a lifetime of experiences. Even the *mundane* or regular activities of everyday life have the capacity to prove significant in shaping the lifetime soundtrack.

Making musical memories in everyday life

The concept of everyday life is an idea that has been central to the inclusion of music in sociological studies. Tia DeNora's *Music in Everyday Life* (2000) presents a series of case studies examining the everyday "ordinary" use of music, its contribution to identity construction and to our personal and social routines. While other music sociologists such as Simon Frith had helped pave the way for the establishment of this area, DeNora's was the first ethnographic, in-depth exposition on the role played by music in facilitating and accompanying everyday social activities. While DeNora's book stimulates discussion on the role of music in daily routines, it refers to memory only fleetingly, briefly describing the tendency for music to become associated with autobiographical memories of people, places or senses of temporality. Despite this, she is often cited by authors of memory-related studies, typically in opening paragraphs that establish the legitimacy of the study of music interacting with features of the human condition, such as identity and autobiographical memory (e.g. Anderson 2004; van Dijck 2006; Bull 2007; Janata *et al.* 2007; Gabrielsson 2011).

The significance of DeNora's work does not necessarily lie in a contribution to the study of memory, but rather in her treatment of music as a routinely encountered, yet socially and individually meaningful, aspect of experience. DeNora effectively introduces the duality of music and the concept of the "everyday", which can be seen as the most appropriate temporal context for the creation of and reflection upon musical memories on an individual level; this prefaces the frequent reflection upon her work in studies concerning music and memory. The importance of experience in everyday life is central to the current research, because it is our responses to music in daily situations that form autobiographical memory. Our seemingly routine experiences with music can easily become intense and deeply moving, guided by the circumstances of listening or making music. Whether mundane or profound, our musical encounters become intertwined with events large and small over a lifetime, eventually becoming canonized into a lifetime soundtrack that accompanies autobiographical memories.

A specific example that connects memory and music in the everyday comes from Hays and Minichiello (2005) who investigated the emotional, social, intellectual and spiritual role that music plays in the lives of older Australians. Much like the interviews carried out for the current research, the life experience of participants was emphasized, and the role of music within that experience was questioned. Hays and Minichiello asked participants about the importance of music as a feature of their everyday life. They found that their cohort used music to aid well-being spiritually, emotionally and socially. Significantly, the authors acknowledged that "when people listened to particular choices of music, they recalled events and experiences in their life along with the emotions associated with those experiences" (2005: 441). This process is reflected in what Hays and Minichiello note as their most important finding, which was that "the participants' narratives of the meaning of music provides [sic] the ability to construct meaning in their lives. The meaning was directly related to his or her life experiences and emotional needs" (449). This therefore gives credence to the idea that a reflection upon a lifetime soundtrack will conjure memories that often lead the individual to a feeling of validation that their life has been significant and is imbued with meaning.

Collective memory, collective influences

The connections between music and memory can be described through a personal and/or a collective lens. Although this book is mostly interested in the way musical memories manifest for individuals, the spheres of the individual and collective memory are not mutually exclusive. Undoubtedly, music trends and peer listening habits are part of the collective influence that helps to shape the lifetime soundtrack. To define collective memory is problematic; the concept has developed and its applications broadened since its origin in the work of sociologist Maurice Halbwachs in the 1950s. Halbwachs states that collective memory, rather than being simply the sum of an individual's memory, is a greater concept that works upon, within and beyond that memory to "reconstruct an image of the past which is in accord, in each epoch, with the predominant thoughts of a society" (1952/1992: 40). In broad accounts of collective or social memory, such as that offered by Misztal (2003: 25), collective memory is defined as "the representation of the past, both the past shared by a group and the past that is collectively commemorated, that enacts and gives substance to the group's identity, its present conditions and its vision of the future". This definition expands on Halbwachs' work by categorizing collective memory as a function of a community's identity. Since the publication of Halbwachs' ideas, scholars have argued for the division of the concept into narrower discourses that describe more effectively the nuances of collective memories. Subsequently, terms such as social memory (reflecting Halbwachs' definition), generational memory, cultural memory and political memory have come to be widely used in theories of memory and society (Assmann 2006).

Where music is concerned, there have been few attempts to connect cultural or collective memory with the opinions of individuals. One exception is found in Strong's grunge ethnography (2011: 65), in which one-to-one interviews highlight the role of the individual, despite the dominant focus of the study being the collective subculture who share "a common understanding of grunge, without having come into contact with each other". This shared appreciation of the genre nonetheless prompts personal reactions and associations that are often maintained in autobiographical memory. Perhaps the most prominent research to attempt to bridge the gap between collective and personal musical memories comes in the form of van Dijck's (2006) study of reactions to an audience-polled "Dutch Top 2000" radio countdown. The concept of subcultures is again inherent in the connection between participants in the poll, who have an affinity with each other through shared music preferences, and in some cases a shared interpretation of a song's meaning. Importantly, van Dijck states that autobiographical memory for music must be embedded in larger social contexts and that musical memories "become manifest at the intersection of personal and collective memory and identity" (358). This can be seen as evident in the lifetime soundtrack, which, though unique to individuals, is often influenced by music shared by others. The soundtrack can therefore be viewed as something of an interface – a record of musical experience that is at once autobiographical and shared by many people. This point will become clearer throughout Chapter 2, in which I discuss the beginning of the lifetime soundtrack as something constructed from mediated music and re-interpreted experiences rather than being solely generated by an individual.

Conclusion

This chapter has outlined a range of ways in which memories are created and the contexts in which they may be recalled. Of significance is the relationship between the lifetime soundtrack and McAdams's concept of the life story: the discourses that come to light when reflecting on our soundtracks are likely to mirror many, though not all, aspects of life where music rubs up against the activities of everyday life. This temporal domain is a critical part of looking into how the lifetime soundtrack functions – the daily connections we make between self, music and the environment around us are what shape our musical memories, sorting the important moments from the less useful, and enhancing existing connections by reflexive listening practices. The functions of autobiographical memory are called into play, for this kind of memory is designed to serve us in daily life. The question of why *music* persists in our memories should not be dismissed as fruitless flashbacks; rather, our personal music cache acts as a resource to remind us of who we are, and what we've experienced. Reflecting on our actions through music allows the partial replication of thoughts and feelings to occur, in ways that cannot be accessed through other forms of memory aids. Whether through vivid or cloud memory, music relates back particular experience, though our evaluation of memories changes to align with current attitudes and subsequent experiences with the passing of time. The contents of the lifetime soundtrack may also present a challenge to the parameters of autobiographical memory, because music is often shared, if not among just a few, through to hundreds of thousands of listeners. Following the thoughts of van Dijck (2006), memory for music, especially popular music, sits at the intersection of collective and personal memory, which in turn positions the lifetime soundtrack as individually created but socially influenced.

Notes

1. The participant has referred to "Victory in Europe Day", which marks officially the end of the Second World War, celebrated in Australia on 8 May 1945. Given his description, it is more likely that the participant is referring to V.J. Day (Victory over Japan Day, also called V.P. Day, for Victory in the Pacific Day), which occurred on 14 August 1945.

2. This refers to the national public radio and news broadcaster, Australian Broadcasting Corporation.

3. A traditional song with gestures implied in the lyrics.

2 Foundations and Development of the Lifetime Soundtrack

Musical memories have so far been established as highly individual, able to be formed and recalled at just about any time in day-to-day life. And while each instance could be considered on its own merit and meaning, it is more effective to introduce the framework of the lifetime soundtrack to allow for the discussion of musical memories as part of a greater continuum of auto-biographical memory. The structure and contents of the lifetime soundtrack develops over time; in similar ways to personal psychological development, the foundations are laid early in life. A lifetime soundtrack is framed by the contextualized experiences of each individual, and as such it is unique to them. On the other hand, the creation of that soundtrack often stems from interaction with others, whether the activity is participatory, such as singing, or passive, comprising forms of listening. The soundtrack develops concurrently with the evolution of autobiographical memory in young children, both of which are typically guided by adults in spaces of safety and reflection, such as the home.

Temporal, spatial and social contexts continue to influence the soundtrack as it develops – but the ways in which they are present in early life are particularly important in shaping our longer-term preferences for engaging with and valuing music in its varying forms. The stage of "early life" refers predominantly to childhood, which is characterized by dependence on others – where choices are often made for, rather than by, an individual. One such choice that is often made for children regards their sound environment: exposure to music is almost entirely determined by caregivers, where children often receive their musical education through purposeful introduction (e.g. singing lullabies to aid sleep, nursery rhymes or children's music for entertainment) or mediated exposure, where children are present while music is played for the purposes of others (e.g. adult-oriented music, social occasions, shopping malls, etc.). Typically, then, the beginnings of the lifetime soundtrack will be shaped by others while independence and the growing ability to express preference become significant agents to influence the soundtrack in times to come.

This chapter is presented in two sections: in the first, I explore the network of care that imparts music experience to young people, especially families, and the ways in which the lifetime soundtrack begins through contact with others. The initial and often serendipitous experiences an individual has with music can create strong mnemonic associations, not only with caregivers but also with the place of these interactions. The chapter then turns to a discussion of the home as the prevailing location in which the introduction of music occurs. Commonalities of the home, family (or family-like contexts), and the presence or absence of music technologies are presented here, where they indicate the soundtrack is open to influence rather than necessarily being self-determined. Participants' narratives suggest that in childhood and adolescence, practices of music listening and music-making with others share a balance that is encountered less frequently in later life. This chapter will establish the typical foundations of the lifetime soundtrack as characterized by the space of the home, mediated by family members in the early years of life. It also raises questions about the influence of taste and gender, and the role of portable technologies in facilitating different modes of listening that help construct the lifetime soundtrack.

Musical memory, influence and mediation

The temporal frame of a lifetime can be split into "life stages" (as per Erikson 1959), and can include the labels childhood, adolescence, young adulthood, adulthood, middle age, retirement age, old age or elderly, where each stage represents variations in mental and physical advancement or decline. The stages of earlier and later life often present more challenges or points of interest for researchers working in memory and have been the focus of a good deal of scholarship that explores both the development and decline of memory. In this research, participants could often easily describe memories for music that originated at a young age, which is significant in understanding the origins of the lifetime soundtrack. These memories are essentially autobiographical; however, they diverge from adult recollections in a number of ways: firstly, because children are still developing psychologically, and secondly, because they are often co-constructed with an adult. The cognitive ability to create and reflect on narratives of autobiographical memory is developed throughout the life course but begins in childhood. Child psychologists believe autobiographical memories begin to be verbalized by children at about three years of age (Nelson 1993; Rubin 2000) and are cultivated through a process of parental guidance (Nelson and Fivush 2004; Fivush 2008; Reese and Fivush 2008). Fivush explains that young children learn how to recall and retell memories via parentally guided reminiscing, typically though discussion of recent events (2008: 53). Developing this kind of memory involves the re-telling of the surrounding visual and aural environment with prompts from a parent or caregiver (e.g. "and then what happened?"), and also encompasses many "first experiences" that subsequently make early life a significant time of memory production. Significantly, in discussing past events with parents, children learn which aspects of memories are important to exchange (Reese and Fivush 2008: 204), and how much detail to provide to others about certain events, which can in turn influence the richness of autobiographical memories for childhood (Reese and Farrant 2003). Such conversations constitute a sharing of memory that allows children to reflect on their own account of an event, their own feelings and beliefs, which eventually leads to a development of self-identity and memories that are significant to and about oneself (Reese and Fivush 2008: 206). When we imagine how this process might play out when music is added to memories, it is easy to see how the beginnings of musical memories that can persist into adulthood are created.

Music may start to make up some of the aural aspects of memory narratives as children both become aware of, and are exposed to, music in various forms. The practice of listening to or sharing music between caregivers and children is similar in some ways to the parent-child interaction that develops autobiographical memory in young children. In line with Bourdieu's concept of *habitus* (1984), children are socialized in the family environment to understand and value music in certain ways, which can have a relationship to socio-economic class. The experience of music for children is regularly mediated by caregivers, in terms of the genre of music, whether the music is used purposefully or in the background, the technology used to listen, the length of time, and the frequency of music engagement. In some scenarios, caregivers may choose to play music that has personal significance to them: it is part of their lifetime soundtrack. Repeated listening can suggest to children the level of importance this music has for that person, even if a discussion of the music never takes place. Similar to the reflection practices in which caregivers guide the creation of autobiographical memories, the selection of music played in the presence of young people can guide not only their musical preferences later in life but can also shape the evaluation of musical memories as significant. Just as one's first memories are mediated by parental help in creating narratives, the lifetime soundtrack is founded in mediated listening practices where first memories of music may in fact incorporate elements of the caregiver's soundtrack.

The meaning of early musical memories that feature in the lifetime soundtrack may not fully emerge for some time. Though memories can be created from a young age, it is not until late adolescence that we become able to critically reflect on the importance of memories to our sense of self and our place in the world around us. Habermas and Bluck call this "autobiographical reasoning" (2000), the processes of which are related to the struggles with self-identity that are often encountered at this life stage and continue into early adulthood. This chapter draws on participants' memories of childhood in the first instance; however, the discourses of adolescence begin to arise where interview participants describe greater independence in music preferences, looking to an extending network of people outside the family who are providing influence for both their musical taste and their soundtrack.

Early life and the music of caregivers

Typically, the early years of a person's life are spent in the company of their family, with the majority of waking hours spent in and around the home. Increasingly, however, these circumstances are becoming diversified – the idea of family need not adhere to a popularized twentieth-century Western ideal of two heterosexual parents with two or three children, living under one roof, with a further assumption that the dwelling has been mortgaged, rather than leased or shared. The concept of family varies between cultures and continues to change over time. The "nuclear" structure has been challenged by alternatives such as *de facto* co-habitation, same-sex and queer relationships, adopted children, and childless families (Cutas and Chan 2012: 1–2). Recent changes in some Western legislations have also come to reflect that traditional relationships between family members are no longer restricted to those that are biological (e.g. parent to child), monogamous, or heterosexual, thereby redefining the "family" at large (Bala and Bromwich 2002; Almond 2006). With these issues in mind, the concept of family as it used within this book is a loose approximation and refers inclusively to the caregivers and peers comprising the household relationships described by interviewees.

Young children are likely to experience music that is mediated by caregivers until they develop the social and cultural skills to select their own music (Krumhansl and Zupnick 2013). This early mediatory practice provides the beginning of an individual's personal memory for music. The events that occur during time spent absorbing pre-selected music can resonate with an individual throughout their lifetime, something described in ethnographic research of musicians by Bennett (2000) and Cohen (1991) where parents' record collections stimulated a life-long obsession with particular music. The physical boundaries of domestic spaces allow repeated and varied interactions between family members to form a layered sense of experience with familiar music that develops over time. The significance of caregivers and other family members in mediating music is evident in the memories of participants recounting their experiences with music as young children. Of course, while there is a great deal of music specifically written and recorded for children, this makes up only part of what a young person might hear on a daily or weekly basis. Rather, the role of the caregiver is often that of an incidental mediator, the music is for them, not necessarily for the children, but this does not preclude childrens' engagement:

> A pretty early memory was like the road trips and stuff ... before
> that maybe it was Mum doing the housework and I wouldn't have
> been old enough to be at school but she'd be, I'm trying to remem-
> ber what she'd listen to but, like thinking back now really cheesy
> sort of stuff but um, that's a memory I guess, just at home with
> Mum (Ryan, age 20).

Ryan's memory for his mother is associated with music from an early age.
The use of music in this narrative is described as an accompaniment to chores
and was probably not intended to be a prime source of entertainment for
mother or child. Though the memory is not detailed, and the music is non-
specific, the association continues to resonate with Ryan over time.

As young people mature, the dynamic between passive and active listening
to mediated music changes. The family, and particularly those in prime caregiver positions, has been well-established in the literature as holding significant influence over the future cultural preferences of their children. Whether
through the purposeful instillation of these preferences or simply through its
presence within a household, parents are highly influential in shaping young
people's perceptions and tastes (Mohr and DiMaggio 1995; Nagel and Ganzeboom 2002; ter Bogt *et al.* 2011). This process of "family socialization"
can subsequently influence the musical taste of children in their company,
whose subsequent preferences tend to mirror those of parents. Examples of
this process were sometimes described by parents:

> I can remember, [my ex-husband] just left and I said to the girls,
> "we're going to paint upstairs, we're going to paint the upstairs
> room" and [my daughter's] going "I really want a blue room", so,
> great! Cracked on Shirley Bassey and here we are – we've got the
> blue paint and we're singing away. And it's funny because my girls
> idolize Shirley Bassey because they, you know, they must remember
> me singing it incessantly at times (Angela, age 43).

Angela describes the recordings of Shirley Bassey as a significant part of
her lifetime soundtrack; by referring to the frequency of her use of Shirley
Bassey especially in coping emotionally during her divorce, she recognizes
the heightened exposure of her daughters to this music and their ostensibly
strong relationship to it as a consequence. In other tales, people spoke of the
relationship they had not just with their parents but with a physical music collection. This includes the act of "choosing" though the options are confined
by the nature of the collection:

> You know certainly [as a child] that was a bit of a focus, you know
> lifting stuff out of the parents' record collection like Simon and
> Garfunkel's *Bridge Over Troubled Water* or, other things like that,

> [it's] the music that you're presented with rather than music you've
> actually sought out (Paul, age 42).

Paul's habits demonstrate an essential method through which musical preferences can be passed on to successive generations. Unable to really seek out music independently beyond the home, Paul was content to enjoy that which was familiar and enjoyable to his perception. His love for Simon and Garfunkel persisted over his life, with mention of the duo cropping up several times in our interview.

The prevalence of mediating music preferences suggests that parents or caregivers play a significant role in shaping their children's lifetime soundtrack and are especially responsible for the formative years of their music experience. The foundation for the lifetime soundtrack is built up through mediated listening, with the choice of engagement largely limited for the individual. Even as young people are on the cusp of autonomy in terms of music choice, they might first explore more deeply their parents' collection, which often acts as a starting point on their own taste journey:

> It was probably when I was around 11 or 12 I started listening to
> it, buying a lot more albums and that's when I became really interested in music, and varied types. I remember, you just get into popular music when you're around 11 or 12 and then around the age
> of 15 I was listening to all my Dad's CDs, so going back and listening to classic rock, classical music, jazz, ska, punk, all those kind of
> things. I remember when Napster[1] came out I wouldn't download
> the newest songs, I'd be downloading things like Don McLean and
> Meatloaf and that kind of varied stuff (Will, age 26).

In similar ways to Paul, Will recalls going through CDs (rather than vinyl records) from his father's collection. Will speaks about his age in this memory with a sense of importance, acknowledging an awareness of his development in taste. Both Will and Paul engaged in purposeful listening activities where they actively chose to listen to music with the awareness that such music was part of their caregiver's musical preferences. In making the choice to listen to this music, these individuals are actively integrating music that is potentially in their parents' soundtrack into their own. This is the beginning of an exercise in agency for young people, where familiar music, once mediated, is now engaged with purposefully. It is at this point when the music may take on new meanings as it is listened to in a refreshed mind-set.

The sharing of soundtracks can also be influential through the bonds they help create between generations. A significant example of parental sharing and mediation spans three generations in Jeremy's family. His narrative is an example of a very early memory connecting music and family:

> I think one of the earliest memories I have, it's connected to music … 'cause I remember the house we were in – I would have had to have been probably five or six and we used to play a game with Mum and Dad and my brother called "monsters in the dark" – it was basically hide and seek at night with all the lights turned off. And Dad would play, put on the record player and he'd put on Black Sabbath's 'Iron Man', which had a scary beginning to it, it starts out and it goes "I am IRON MAN" and that would be the song, we'd have to go – I was always scared so Dad would crawl around on all fours and I'd be on his back, clutching onto his back and we'd go find my Mum and my brother … So I've actually introduced [my young son] to 'Iron Man' now and he asks for it all the time (Jeremy, age 36).

From grandfather to father to son, Black Sabbath's 'Iron Man' has been mediated through two parental soundtracks and probably feature in all three individuals' lifetime soundtracks. The cyclical nature of the lifetime soundtrack is highlighted here, drawing similarities with oral folk music traditions in which music is passed down through generations. In this way, mediated music can become the basic referent to which subsequent material of the lifetime soundtrack is compared. The idea that familiarity and knowledge of music is passed on between family generations has been traced in music psychology in studies of the "reminiscence bump", which describes a trend for people to remember music released during their childhood through to young adulthood, but also suggests that a significant proportion of individuals' memories are associated with music that was popular when their parents were young adults (Krumhansl and Zupnick 2013). In the above narrative, this bump is amplified two-fold, because 'Iron Man' is originally apart of "grandad's" lifetime soundtrack. As time goes on, it will be interesting to see how popular music, which itself is constantly undergoing genre and decade-based revivals, filters through soundtracks generationally, potentially on a grand, global scale.

The home as a centre of musical interaction

Already in this chapter there has been reference to domestic spaces within the home; however, this concept is rather broad and requires further definition. The concept of home is not universally understood, especially where Western conceptions of home tend to align this concept with a physical house (Bowlby *et al.* 1997), though "home" might also be thought of in a spiritual sense. For the purposes of discussion here, home is a "place", both geographically and metaphorically, and is often a hub of social interaction. Hudson (2006: 627), states that "'places' can be thought of as complex entities, ensembles of material objects, people and systems of social relationships embodying distinct cultures and multiple meanings, identities and practices". To extend on this we can look to Mallett (2004: 63), who says that "home is place but it is also a space inhabited by family, people, things and belongings – a familiar if not comfortable space where particular activities and relationships are lived." Perhaps most pertinent in thinking about the home in relation to music, Sixsmith (1986: 281–82) defines home as a centre of emotional significance and belonging, and a medium of self-expression and identity. These definitions imply that a typical family home embodies systems of social relationships within physical bounds; the kinds of interactions that take place within the home may differ significantly to those actioned in other places. For physical, social and emotional reasons, the home has high potential to become a significant theme in autobiographical memories, particularly musical ones.

In his writing on significant events and the visual nature of memories, Pillemer (1998: 96) refers to the visualization of significant physical places in memory as "memory landmarks". This is a crucial component in the reconstruction of memory; Pillemer explains that "constructing a coherent, temporally ordered life history depends on having access not only to the meaning of momentous past events, but also to the imagistic components of personal event memories" (ibid.). From this perspective, the recognition of places, such as "the home", work schematically, where familiarity with place can draw together memories with a common geographical feature, a template on which memory can be temporally and physically located. As a common and often revisited concept for participants, home as a locus for memories proves to be both enduring and transient. Likewise, the memories for people within these places are malleable: even people of significance or of traditionally influential positions (e.g. mother or father), along with those whose permanence is felt only briefly, fluctuate in dominance throughout a lifetime.

Early musical memories can involve participation in making music as well as listening. For both older and younger interview participants, home was often a location of musical participation and interaction. Music-making, as opposed to listening, can find slightly different pathways into memory due to its use of different parts of the brain and body. Tony's narrative, below, is one of his very first memories associated with music, though he happens to be the one generating the tune:

> The first thing I can absolutely remember was me and my sister, wandering round the house singing 'Yes Sir, She's My Baby'[2] [sings] and we just somehow or other, without really meaning to, ended up being able to sing that in harmony with each other, and that was just something we obviously absorbed from what we'd heard you know ... I was probably three and she was probably five ... and once we'd demonstrated we could do it you know, when our parents' friends came round or rellies came round "sing, sing!" so we'd sing at people, do a little performance, you know. So, I remember that, um, as being incredibly important (Tony, age 62).

Aside from the impressive musicality evident in this narrative, it is also interesting to note the way Tony describes this occurrence coming about: in acknowledging that he and his sister had "absorbed" their surroundings, this narrative exposes the significance of cultural mediation between music environment and children. In our interview, Tony also described his parents as musical, with both playing in ensembles outside of the home, which may have been an encouraging factor in this early show of musicianship. This narrative further exemplifies not only the reception of mediated music but also the perception and reproduction of musical skills that can play out in the home.

Some older participants described an era when the family frequently made their own entertainment with music they performed themselves. The narratives below illustrate certain aspects of life in rural Queensland as well as the developing capital city of Brisbane in the 1940s and 50s:

> Well again you did have people in the small town that could play the piano, but that meant that one person stayed at the piano the whole night, whereas we had the Pianola and everyone came to our place. Mum and Dad, we had an old Queenslander with big verandas, and we danced there on a Sunday night with the Pianola, and everyone could use the Pianola, all you had to do was pump your feet (Bea, age 81).

> Well we used to have sing-a-longs as a family, we didn't go out to party, people came, you didn't go out to eat at that time, well I s'pose some people did but we didn't go out to eat. People came in for dinner and you'd sit around afterwards and have small talk for a while, but then the lid would come open on the piano and you'd have sing-a-longs (Hazel, age 72).

The emphasis in these memories from Bea and Hazel is on the collective experience of making music with family and friends in the home. As Bea says, it could be an inclusive activity where everyone could join in, strengthening the ties between memories of loved ones and musical experiences. Although listening technologies in the home were available, they were not realistically priced for many families in the country during and after World War Two. These narratives give insight into typical additions to lifetime soundtracks of individuals prior to the wide availability of recorded music as a form of entertainment. The home is integral to the formation of these memories, either in one's own, or in that of family or friends' as the prime location of making music together.

Live music plays an equally important part in the lifetime soundtrack as recorded music and is significant because of the ephemeral nature of the experience – no two performances are ever exactly the same, and so the memories captured in the moment can be particularly special. Below, Ron described a unique scenario in which he experienced live music performed by professional musicians in his childhood home:

> What would happen is my brother then became a professional musician and travelled with what they called the JC Williamson Orchestra that did all the musicals that came up the east coast of Australia from Victoria to Cairns, and they stopped in Melbourne, Sydney, Brisbane, and sometimes Toowoomba ... but mostly stop[ped] in Brisbane ... So in my early years at Moggill[3] he'd have ballet people come out, and the orchestra and he'd put on a barbeque at home. So ... I would have opera singers on a Friday night, the best opera singers that would travel in Australia would sing in our lounge room. And then the best jazz players of the time, there's this bloke called Ronnie Milner, he was playing trumpet in the Brisbane Symphony Orchestra but he was also a jazz player so this is late 60s ... oh, mid to late 60s, so it put me anywhere between 12 and 16 years of age. And that was a huge influence, was having these people. And that diversified my interest in music from semi-classical to jazz, and you could have it all in the one evening (Ron, age 59).

What makes this experience such a vivid memory for Ron over any other kind of live music performance is the venue: the family home provides familiar scenery present in memories of typical domestic activities; however, performers from travelling Symphony Orchestras within one's living room is most certainly not a typical experience. This novelty helps to reinforce the importance of the experience for Ron, remaining a crucial encounter in his autobiographical memory.

Private listening: bedrooms and radio in memories of the Australian home

Ron's experience of live performance in the home is uncommon, but finds tangential roots in the era of home radios, where broadcasters brought elements of national and international developments, including news, sports and music, streaming into domestic life. The growing influence of the radio was felt in Australian homes after the establishment of the Australian Broadcasting Corporation in 1932. The radio became extremely important in Australian daily life, and for many participants the radio was a crucial medium in the creation of musical memories. As a government-funded station that continues to have the widest broadcast range, including the rural and remote areas of Australia, ABC radio provided people mostly with information – which was critical especially during the war years – and various forms of entertainment including sports coverage (especially cricket), drama serials, and music. Though not all households could afford a radio until well beyond the mid-twentieth century, if there was a radio in the house there would usually be only one, positioned in the living areas for family listening. As Frith observes: "It was radio which transformed the use of domestic space, blurring the boundary between the public and the private, idealizing the family hearth as the site of ease and entertainment, establishing the rhythm of everydayness" (2002: 41). Collected interview narratives depict the radio as a regular accompaniment to life, comprising part of both personal and family listening time.

Arrow (2005) traced the influence of the widely popular Australian radio serial *Blue Hills* on domestic life. She asked the general public to write to her with their memories of this serial, noting that "the letters are not just about people's memories of the pleasures of listening to *Blue Hills* … memories of *Blue Hills* frame listeners' memories of childhood, marriage, family, domesticity and daily life" (p. 306). This is reflected in one of my own interviews with a participant named George, who also told how the theme song of *Blue Hills* features in his own memory of domestic life:

> When we lived on a research station[4] in New Guinea about ten miles out of Lai, and I was working at the office and I would go home for lunch, and at lunchtime on the ABC Radio National they'd play *Blue Hills*. They'd have *Blue Hills*, and the signature tune [sings]. I can still remember that and that reminds me of having lunch at home with [my wife] in Papua New Guinea, the signature tune of *Blue Hills* … You'd have the one o'clock news and they have the pips to signify that it was one o'clock and then they'd have the tune for *Blue Hills* (George, age 66).

The sounds of this era are important to George, with the tune of *Blue Hills* triggering a multitude of memories from this time in his life. This musical memory includes sounds outside of the music itself, with reference to the "pips" that would immediately precede it. Just as described in Arrow's collected narratives (2005), the theme tune signified a time of respite for working individuals to enjoy a break from work accompanied by the serial.

Originally, music was played sparingly on ABC radio: listeners needed to wait for set times in the week when music was scheduled for broadcast. Part of the strong attachment to radio described by participants could be attributed to a novelty factor of listening to music on the radio. This is evident in a story from an older participant, Vincent, who spent his school years in a strict boarding facility; his memories exemplify not only an alternative memory locus to the "home" but also structured listening opportunities provided by the radio:

> Because we were seniors we were given the privilege of listening every Sunday night to the "Hit Parade". And some of the songs, when I hear, songs like, [sings] *"C'mon kid, c'mon kid hit him with the left and right / C'mon kid, c'mon how were they to know it was*

the kid's last fight"[5] takes me back. I just made a note of some of them I could remember: 'Via Con Dios' [sings] these are hit songs of the period ... 'Down by the Riverside', 'Jealousy' [sings], those are the sorts of songs that were on the "Hit Parade" in those days. And whenever afterwards I heard one of those anywhere, I'd be under the mosquito net at Nudgee [College], and then you'd doze off and away (Vincent, age 77).

Though Vincent's memory is set in a dormitory, it functions like a bedroom, where the other boys and housemaster act as temporary family. While he would have returned to his kin in semester breaks, Vincent's term-time family would have most likely been his peer group. Hence this memory still informs the lifetime soundtrack, resounding with the foundations thereof: despite its occurrence in later adolescence, the substitution of the boarding college for "home" and his fellow pupils for "family" still comprise a hub for memory creation.

As the availability and demand for music grew over the mid-twentieth century, so too did the growth of personal music collections and the duplication of technologies, such as the radio or stereo, within private listening environments of teenagers: the bedroom. According to McRobbie and Garber (1976), this space was a physical centre for teen-oriented cultures, especially for girls post-1945. The bedroom offers unique experience for interaction with music that, as Baker (2004) describes, allows an exploration of gendered identity. The significance of listening in private spaces was evidenced particularly in the narratives of older and younger women:

I can remember the night that 'Waterloo' won the Eurovision song contest. Cos I was listening to it on this little yellow radio that ... my mum had bought in Singapore and I was in bed at night-time with the little radio, tucked up listening to the Eurovision song contest in Germany or wherever it was broadcast from, and ABBA won [with] 'Waterloo', so I do remember that[6] (Vivian, age 51).

I was obsessed with [radio station] B105 ... completely obsessed, I listened to it all day, and I used to call up at night, for like all the competitions. I used to listen to "Kyle and Jackie O", "The Hot 30" ... I used to listen religiously, every night I'd listen to the entire three-hour show, like, just sit in my room. Sometimes I would write down [the lyrics to] songs. And they were just terrible pop songs, like I probably wouldn't even remember them now, but occasionally an old pop song will come on and I'll strangely know all of the words (Stella, age 22).

The age difference between Stella and Vivian is indicative of the sustained importance of the radio through to the late twentieth century. The activity of listening to music alone or with friends in the confines of a bedroom often means that the experience becomes highly personalized. In these scenarios, people are able to spend more time listening to music than would be possible in shared spaces within the home, contributing to a pattern of increased engagement with music associated with teenage life and young adulthood, where youth use music reflexively to explore their worlds socially and emotionally. An increased investment in music, especially in familiar spaces like the bedroom, can significantly impact the lifetime soundtrack, helping to define time and place in long-term memory.

With the development of the transportable transistor radio in the 1950s, radio could become a personal, individual experience, and moreover, a mobile one. This was reflected in the following narrative about Radio Luxembourg from participant Dennis, who spent his formative years in the United Kingdom:

> Up to [age] 13, I was in England and that's when I remember the early stages of music, 'cause that's when Radio Luxembourg started, I don't know if you remember that, the first radio stations. I was only young and living in that, near the coast of England ... [we] used to pick up the radio signal from Radio Luxembourg[7] which started off with early popular music like The Beatles ... Dave Clark Five, all that really early English music and I remember actually listening to it on our little transistor when I was only 13 or less than that, probably 11 or 12 years old. That was my first experience with music, so that was quite interesting because I was quite young, I was awake to when it first really started, popular music (Dennis, age 61).

The music played on Radio Luxembourg was influential for many young people around the world, Dennis included, although it is only in retrospect that the participant can recognize the significance of the experience.

In recounting musical influence in childhood, George described the frequency with which he would listen to the radio for the popular music of the time in a shared bedroom:

> I did have the bad habit of listening to the radio while I studied, much to the annoyance of my brother Johnny ... and I remember um, my favourite radio station at night was 2UW in Sydney, and the guy had an American accent, he was "Grant Walker, Grant Walker" and he used to be – his signature was 2UWW it had the echo on it, the reverb – and he used to play the latest, all the stuff from the States and everything so, I would just have that on, always had music on while I studied (George, age 66).

George's habit of listening to the radio in childhood carried on into adult life, and as for many others it became ingrained as a daily accompaniment to other activities. The technology of transistor radios plays a large part in private listening practices of this era, where these newly mobile devices allowed teens to listen to music away from the collective family-oriented listening that was more likely to be playing in other areas of the home.

Rising concurrently with the popularity of radio was recorded, re-playable music; playback technologies such as the phonograph, the cassette, and more recently, the CD and the mp3 file have helped maintain music's place in the home, though the radio is still commonly used. Though the radio was prevalent in many childhood memories, other mediums such as the record, tape and CD were also mentioned, though less frequently:

> [Hearing David Cassidy or the Osmonds] takes me back to when I was a teenager you know. I would listen to them in my bedroom you know or on like the little cassette players or you know, cos they were the big things back then, cassettes (Robyn, age 52).

As the physicality of music technology lessens over time, the ways in which music dominates a room or space will change the interaction. Similarly, the ways in which we interact with music through touch is becoming more customized and personalized. These dynamic aspects of music interaction will continue to impact on where and how the lifetime soundtrack is created for people in the future, especially in the stages of adolescence and young adulthood.

Music in the car

So far, I have established that the home is one of the most common places within which the lifetime soundtrack takes shape, due to the influence of caregivers' music, shared listening environment and the control of this environment. People in this study also commonly recalled the car as being another place where similar listening conditions are imposed. From the use of the transistor radio to the current mp3 technology, participants described music accompanying journeys both long and short. While Bull (2004) and Walsh (2010) explore drivers' attitudes towards solitary listening in the car, only a few participants in the current research had strong memories of listening alone on a journey. More apparent in these narratives were associations between the car as a listening venue and the people, generally family members, within (see also Istvandity 2019).

Typically, narratives incorporating music and cars centred on family road trips and holiday time. Walsh (2010: 214) notes the intentionality of choosing music for extended periods of travel in order to "disrupt the static quality of car habitation", a view that was supported by his interview participants. While this may be the case for adults, children in vehicles are often subject to the music selections of the caregivers or driver:

> And I do remember listening to Hot Chocolate when we were young, as a family going through Tasmania. Through Christmases and stuff like that, when I was probably 11-10, 11 or 12, so that one's just come back. Just remember the albums, like *Hot Chocolate Greatest Hits* and we just had it on in the car the whole time. 'Cause it was all tapes you know, didn't have CDs or anything like that, it was all about tapes at that stage (James, age 41).

> Well [my family] drove from the top of New Zealand to the very bottom of New Zealand when I was like seven and then we left the country [to emigrate to Australia]. We didn't see much down there but we moved to a place called Gore [in the South Island of New Zealand], and the entire way down we listened to Enya, and it was like, repeat, and it was just like, I've never listened to Enya so much, nobody else would have, why would you? ... I think it was like the only tape we had, it was just like constant Enya for an entire country! (Stella, age 22).

Such stories of being at the mercy of their parents' musical mediation are reminiscent of household listening environments. Adults' musical preferences in the car inform and shape younger people's lifetime soundtracks in much the same way as they would within the confines of the family home. Both of the stories above also bemoan the technology of music available at the time – cassette tapes. The use of tapes in the car usually meant listening through all the music on the tape, with the ability to exclusively skip tracks effectively limited. This further intensifies the experience for both Stella and James, in that they were not only confined to a small space with their family members, but were additionally restricted to repeated music over which they had little control.

Singing, or singing to music, is also an effective way of passing the time on long trips. Prior to the 1950s, the main musical entertainment option for families both at home and in the car was to make music together. Having lived through this era, Bea fondly remembers trips from rural Queensland to the capital city Brisbane:

> ... my Mum's name was Kathleen, and we used to sing all the way to Brisbane of course, in the car, but then Dad always sang, ah, for mum [pause, Bea is getting a bit teary] – that's silly. Ah yes, he always sang 'I'll Take You Home Again Kathleen' and Dad always sang that, that was the only song he ever sang, and we all kept quiet in the car while Dad used to sing it. Oh, they had a wonderful married life (Bea, age 81).

In this repeat scenario, Bea's father would command the musical space of the vehicle, if only for one tune – his contribution to singing, whilst singular, was attributed more respect than other family members' songs through the family's silence. Bea's recollection is framed through the perspective of her own life; having married and had children of her own, the respect for her mother and father is maintained in this memory.

Not all memories associated with the car need to involve long trips. Matthew also recalled music accompanying short car trips with his father around Jakarta, Indonesia, which is now in his own lifetime soundtrack:

> My Dad's very religious, and we used to go to this church, the actual parish moved a number of times, but I remember the first church was this old beat up church that was in the middle of the city in Jakarta ... I guess the things that always stood out about going to mass at those times were listening to what my Dad had on tapes. Um so I guess the music that came along with that was ah the album [by] Chick Corea, *Light as a Feather* ... he had some Ry Cooder on there, in his tapes. Wilson Phillips sisters ... I guess for the most part it's positive, ah you know, Dad was always tapping along to it, singing along to it ... but I guess on the other end ... he used to have really bad road rage. So that was the other thing I always remember about driving around with him (Matthew, age 25).

There is a distinct atmospheric difference between short and long car journeys where music is involved. Traffic congestion and other factors lead to a disrupted sensory and temporal space on short city-bound trips, where both the continued momentum of the car and the mental absorption of the music are frequently interrupted. Additionally the driver, characterized by Matthew's father, may facilitate a disrupted focus on the music, calling attention to the environment outside the car on journeys within higher density areas. The immersive nature of the car as a listening environment is observable in all the above car-based narratives, contributing to this space as a prime scenario for the creation of musical memories, and a captive audience for transmission of music between lifetime soundtracks.

Domestic attitudes toward music

> There was no popular music ever played in the house (Ron, age 59).

As mentioned earlier, not only can caregivers be highly influential in shaping cultural preferences, but they may also impart to young people their perceived value of music and acceptable levels of engagement (Kalish and Johnson 1972; Hoge, Petrillo and Smith 1982; Barni *et al.* 2011). Political, religious and social values can be passed on generationally and, as such, the attitudes of caregivers have great influence over beliefs and activities within domestic spaces. The concept of social class is particularly relevant here in relation to cultural values and taste. Widely recognized in sociology, the family socialization process alluded to previously in this chapter is based around a connection between social class and levels of formal education, where higher levels of education are generally thought to encourage a greater interest in aesthetic experiences and high art (DiMaggio and Useem 1978; Bourdieu 1984). However, this factor alone is not responsible for taste in music, which remains a topic of contention particularly in regard to popular music (see, for example, Frith 1998; Peterson and Kern 1996). Certainly, in an Australian context, the link between social class and music taste can be relatively weak – of interest here is the work of Turner and Edmunds (2002), whose engagement with Australian "postwar elite" documented a distinct preference for a range of cultural activities, trending toward low-brow over high-brow tastes. The authors offer that in contemporary Australian society, the link between social class and taste is not straightforward, and patterns in taste are more accurately explained with reference to the particular political and social influences on what is perceived as cultural capital in a national, rather than international, context.

In the context of my participants, a similarity in the perceived value of music between generations was generally evident, though the influence of class was less obvious. The typical process of music mediation involves, to varying degrees, the sharing of values, including an emphasis on things that are not valued. This may result in the purposeful exclusion of music or a certain genre thereof within domestic spaces. It is likely then, though of perhaps less influence than political or religious values, that households in which the value of music is minimized may produce lifetime soundtracks that have little basis in childhood music listening. However, not all interviewees shared detailed memories of childhood relating to music, which could be indicative of a number of things. "Missing" narratives from this life stage could be attributed to trauma, a lack of fond memories from early life and an urge to forget, rather than remember. The way people articulate memories can also be attributed to an introverted or extroverted personality type, so not speaking of memories is not necessarily evidence of a memory shortage. In terms of musical memories, some participants described a lack of music in the home, meaning the beginning of their lifetime soundtrack is sparse or restricted. This was the case for Ron, quoted above, whose father's strict rules about the use of the radio and records has had a long-lasting impact: Ron said he has never developed a liking for popular music, and as a musician himself he could not muster any respect for artists of that genre. Ron's lifetime soundtrack reflects this, comprising mostly jazz and classical music.

The value placed on music as expressed by domestic authority figures can significantly affect the ways in which individuals may interact with music in their adult life. A restriction on activities that involve music may also influence the kind of music experienced at that time of life for an individual, and potentially in the future. In a similar way to Ron, Angela described her childhood experiences with music as somewhat inhibited by the beliefs of her father:

> My Dad was a Mason, so when he would go out on a Friday or Saturday night, that was our time at home to watch whatever *we* wanted on the TV with Mum, so it always seemed to be musicals, Fred Astaire and all that, so I love all those standards ... it was something we did as a ... group of girls together at home on a Saturday night sort of thing. And we'd have like toasted cheese sandwiches so you didn't have to cook dinner (Angela, age 43).

Hearing this music through film became a treat highly prized by Angela, given that much of her other involvement with music was confined to classical instrumental lessons. The additional detail of relinquishing a traditional dinner further emphasizes the way in which these occasions were viewed as a time of leisure. Many of Angela's memories that were recollected during her interview featured the music of older musicals, representing how this constraint shaped her lifetime soundtrack. The effect of domestic attitudes towards music again highlights the cyclical nature of the lifetime soundtrack, suggesting that restricted sharing of the parental soundtrack provides a limited foundation for the lifetime soundtrack of young people.

A theme that arose in many of the childhood stories offered up by participants was that delegation of music "ownership" was often assigned to one parental figure. When music was not being enjoyed as a family, for example, at sing-a-longs, it was often referred to as "Mum's music" or "Dad's music". This pattern further illustrates the range of messages a child might perceive via music mediation. From this perspective, associations between family members and music become routinely observed through physical ownership and the action of "pressing play", as well as the overt enjoyment of the music by that person. The following narratives from Will, Matthew and Stella all designate a family member in their musical recollections:

> My Dad's got ... a real varied taste, there was always music playing er, usually stuff my godfather took the piss out of him for. There was always music on, albums on, all round ... my Dad listens to a lot of music, my Mum likes music but wouldn't sit down and put it on ... so she's definitely not got much of a musical influence (Will, age 26).

> My mother was [into] heavier rock from the 80s onwards, so she was into Deep Purple,[8] was one of the bands I associate with her, we had this best of album which included all sorts of songs ... much heavier sort of stuff but at the same time she liked Kenny Rogers which is a pet hate of mine (Matthew, age 25).

I've like ten thousand songs I associate with my Dad because he used to drive me to school every morning and we'd listen to like CDs, he'd like try and – he actually, actively tried to change me from listening to B105,[9] so ... every week we'd have like a new CD that he'd be like "this is real music", and so all Jimi Hendrix I pretty much associate with my Dad, Randy Newman, Joe Jackson, yeah (Stella, age 22).

These strong associations also demonstrate the kind of influence that the parental soundtrack can have on young people, where they may grow to appreciate or loathe music they grew up with. It is interesting to note that although there were more references to musical associations with the maternal figure, it was often the father's music that was said to have a more significant influence. For example, Will implies that his mother did not hold music as something of high value, and so her opinion of it does not matter as much to him. Matthew, on the other hand, has strong associated memories of both his mother and his father; however, in the quote above he notes that his reaction to his mother's musical taste varied, such that he accepted her preference for Deep Purple (hard rock), but not Kenny Rogers (country). The contrasting gender-oriented discourses between the genres of rock and pop-oriented country ballads may be at the heart of this opinion: whereas rock music presents problematic ideals of masculinity (Bayton 1997; Cohen 1997), the undertones of country crooners such as Kenny Rogers offer somewhat more feminine discourses that may be at odds with Matthew's cultural values. Stella's father was also interviewed, confirming Stella's summation of his soundtrack, which she now shares with him in part.

As stated previously, the influence of this mediation often manifests in the development of taste, which has special influence on the lifetime soundtrack in a number of ways. The above excerpts show how participants identified music, but often they went on to elaborate the impact of this music on their own preferences:

Yeah, yeah my Dad um, played a lot of music, he was into sort of hard rock stuff like 60s [and], 70s hard rock which is sort of what I grew up with, that's formed my interest in the kind of music I like today, and liked as I was growing up as well (Jeremy, age 36).

[My mother] liked a lot of pop music, like early 90s pop was her thing so I guess I listened to a lot of Whitney Houston and she got me into Michael Jackson. That's always I guess a really massive influence on all the music I play and a lot of the music I listen to ... (Matthew, age 25).

> Musical taste? … highly influenced by my father, so favourite band, The Beatles, anything from the 60s and 70s. I am *not* a fan of modern music … my musical tastes are highly influenced by people … so growing up with Dad and the Beatles and the music of the 60s and 70s highly influences what I like now I suppose (Anna, age 18).

The age of these participants suggests the degree to which mediated music can have lasting influence on taste, at least through young to mid adulthood. Though taste is not wholly responsible for the lifetime soundtrack, it can alter the way we react to music that is encountered in daily life, and thereby have some effect on the associations that might be made in memory. Gender is again relevant here, with both male and female participants often preferring "dad's music", over their mother's. Although the topic of gender and music (especially popular music) is widely covered in academic scholarship (e.g. Whiteley 1997, 2000; Cohen 1997) there is limited research on the effects of gender-based music associations on the cultural preferences of young people. The influence of caregivers' music generally has been noted elsewhere (e.g. Mohr and DiMaggio 1995; ter Bogt *et al.* 2011), but in the current context, the association of music with one parent or the other may have implications for how the lifetime soundtrack is shaped, and the mnemonic representations of parents through musical memory.

Sharing beyond caregivers: Siblings and extended family

In early life, family rather than friends often dominate sources of influence over the lifetime soundtrack. In the discussion so far, more attention has been given to parents or caregivers in terms of mediating music experience which may lead to associations in memory. However, siblings – especially older siblings – may also influence the development of listening habits and exposure to different kinds of music by more deliberate acts of sharing. This can be particularly influential as young people approaching their teenage years begin to gain a sense of agency in their cultural taste. Older siblings may have already asserted their agency in terms of music preferences, and may also have the ability and resources to afford music of their own:

> We were influenced by [my brother's] music at home, he was a big jazz fan so we had all the old 33s of Benny Goodman and Bob Crosby … [They were] very heavily jazz influenced from those days, Louis Armstrong. So from you know, first stage of recognition of music from say ten, ah him being 13 years older than me so ten gave him 23 … meant that I was influenced by his music. He was buying records and playing them and that was the sort of thing we listened to (Ron, age 59).

The vinyl record is symbolic in this narrative of the dynamic connection between Ron and his much older brother. Significantly, Ron notes his age as being a dominant factor in his interest in music and the opinion of his brother. An interest in the same music can function as a bonding activity between siblings, as in the description from Stella:

> The first time I went to Singapore, me and my next brother up ... got a little bit of pocket money ... and we put all our money into buying a CD Walkman and the Robbie Williams CD, *Sing When You're Winning* and we used to listen to 'Rock DJ' like constantly on this trip. So we made it a task to learn all the words so that we could sing along with 'Rock DJ' so I associate that specifically with [my brother] and being in Singapore (Stella, age 22).

Stella and her brother (who was also interviewed) shared the ownership of the music and the technology they needed to listen to it, with both siblings investing emotionally in at least one particular track together. The bond between Ron and his brother is somewhat more distanced than that in Stella's story; despite this, the importance of the memory to Ron is indicative of the strength of the association. As established in Chapter 1, the act of sharing music has a social function that is seen here in action. Other research states that in sharing music, we are representing parts of who we are, including personality traits and values (Boer *et al.* 2011), which makes sharing parts of our lifetime soundtrack with others particularly meaningful. That the lifetime soundtrack is consolidated by this activity underscores the continued importance of music in our daily life.

Members of the extended family can also play a part in influencing the foundations of a lifetime soundtrack, by introducing new or different music to the sound environment. Jeremy articulated a vivid description of his first encounter with what would go on to become his favourite band:

> I think that would have been around grade six, I was at my cousin's place and she was a full sort of head banger ... she was listening to Guns N' Roses and she had the 'Paradise City' video clip on TV and I just went "that is awesome!" and to this day Guns N' Roses *Appetite for Destruction* is my favourite album, yeah. And I always remember where I got introduced to it and then I became pretty much obsessed with it (Jeremy, age 36).

Jeremy's narrative hints at a number of factors external to the music that may have added to his first impression. His older cousin had already embraced the culture that went along with late 80s/early 90s rock, which presented a new and perhaps even challenging ideology to Jeremy at the time. This story also marks the prevalence of music videos in the 1980s and beyond; it is possible an added visual element of video clips could add to the contextual significance of music in some lifetime soundtrack memories.

Will was quoted previously as saying that his father's music collection had strongly affected his own music preferences. In the narrative below, he notes how an extended family member added to his experiences with music:

> My godfather's one of those people who buys himself an album a week, so his record collection is phenomenal. I'd always ask him when I was getting into music, when I realized I liked it more and you try to look cool I'd always ask him, because he always knew it. Things like Jeff Buckley, I'd say "I found this" and he'd say "Oh I've had that album for years!" … and when I said I was getting myself into Neil Young he said "I've never been so proud!" kind of thing. So my godfather, like in my early years, never had an influence on my music but now I always try to impress him with my music taste because he knows so much about it (Will, age 26).

Will's description of his godfather suggests that this person was often present in his life and was highly influential in terms of cultural development. Will emphasizes that his godfather was very knowledgeable about music, and that he subsequently wanted to impress him with his own music collection, which also implies that the maintenance of a good relationship between them was important. It's interesting to note too that Will says he was "getting himself into Neil Young": this raises the idea that experimenting with different genres to satisfy a developing taste in music may not only spring from music one has been exposed to, but perhaps also music that might meet the approval of caregivers.

Though the mediation process at the heart of this chapter often occurs in a top-down process, the intergenerational transmission of music into family members' soundtracks can also be affected by the young. Angela describes having limited access to music when she was growing up, finding a broader taste for music as an adult:

> I didn't really have my own sort of music, it was always something that was brought to me by somebody else, that we shared that connection. So, the girls liked [the Spice Girls] so "oh yeah I really like that music" and you join in with it and it becomes something that you have together as a group of girls (Angela, age 43).

The Spice Girls' music forms an important part of Angela's soundtrack especially in relation to her daughters, because it becomes a placeholder for a shared bond at a particular point in time. Interestingly, the influence of children's music in the household has been discussed as affecting both musical experiences and relationships between mothers and their sons and/or daughters, especially where it imposes on everyday life (Morgan, MacDonald and Pitts 2015). This can affect the soundtracks of parents, being typically people in their 30s, 40s and 50s who ostensibly have soundtracks of their own that are now being impacted in unexpected ways. Being very open to influence from others in the way Angela described means that the transfer of tastes in the family unit can be multidirectional, and here points to yet another way in which the lifetime soundtrack can be formed and affected by those around us.

Conclusion

This chapter has examined the relationship between memory and music as it develops throughout childhood, adolescence and early adulthood within the home. The domestic space is shown to be an important site for the creation of memory that is associated with music. In these places, the consumption of music is typically mediated by parents or caregivers, such that early memories of music comprise a sound environment that is beyond the immediate control of the individual, reflecting the musical taste of mediators. In this way, the lifetime soundtrack is initiated by others; preferences and values are shared within families or family-like structures, which provide cultural infrastructure while the individual develops autonomy of taste. This goes some way to influencing the lifetime soundtrack, remembering that the soundtrack is not only composed of music one likes. Personal narratives demonstrate how this mediated music becomes ingrained into memories of childhood and is regularly incorporated into the lifetime soundtrack; domestic sites engender shared musical activity, enlisting the listening technologies of the time to facilitate this engagement. Within the home, and even the car, the presence of a radio or home stereo allows music to permeate shared spaces where the dominance over the technology reflects family hierarchies. Privatization of listening, which often happens in later years, enables sharing between siblings and friends, and one's experience of music begins to broaden. Acts of music-making provide a contrasting level of engagement to listening that further personalizes the integration of music into memory; the continuation of this practice will consequently affect the way these memories are formed and reflected upon, something I will explore in more detail in Chapter 5.

A contrast arises between the collective parameters of sharing music, as is often inescapable in family homes, and the fundamental property of autobiographical memories as personal interpretations of experience. The act of sharing music – which continues to be a force influencing the lifetime soundtrack well beyond childhood – is embedded in social habits and contexts, based on a shared sensibility (van Dijck 2006). It would be almost impossible for one to evade the influence of others, not to mention the uninvited strains of music encountered in everyday life. Further, music in one person's lifetime soundtrack is likely to be present in the soundtracks of others; no matter how seemingly obscure, the likelihood that one or more of the tunes in your soundtrack is completely unique is rather low. What is unlikely, however, is the similarity in your interpretation of that music and the significance of associated memory to the experiences of someone else. So, as van Dijck contends, while the music might belong to a collective discourse (2006), the memory belongs to the individual: this makes the lifetime soundtrack a hybrid formation in its most immature forms, but with the passage of time, the canon of personal musical memories becomes so intimately intertwined with aspects of personality, identity and expression, that it is ultimately held by the individual to be singularly theirs.

Notes

1. "Napster" is an online service for peer-to-peer file sharing, established in 1999. Originally, the service of file sharing provided by Napster comprised copyright infringement, and after legal struggles the company closed down and re-opened as a legal online music store.

2. Composed by Walter Donaldson and Gus Kahn, 1925.

3. A suburb of Brisbane, Queensland.

4. George was a scientific researcher for a significant portion of his working life.

5. Refers to 'The Kid's Last Fight' by Frankie Laine, 1954.

6. In 1974, the band ABBA won the Eurovision Song Contest with their song 'Waterloo'. The contest was held in Brighton, UK.

7. Radio Luxembourg was one of the first commercial radio stations to broadcast offshore to the United Kingdom. Established in 1933, it offered an alternative to strict BBC programming that pervaded the UK, and was considered an illegal broadcast station under wireless licensing laws (sometimes referred to as "pirate radio"). Significantly, in the 1950s and 60s Radio Luxembourg targeted a teenage audience, principally playing the popular music of the era. This allowed millions of young Britons access to popular music that was denied them by the BBC up until the launch of its own youth-oriented station, Radio 1, in 1967. Ironically, a number of popular DJs who worked for Radio Luxemburg and other pirate radio stations, such as Radio Caroline, subsequently went on to work for Radio 1.

8. Deep Purple was most influential in the early to mid-1970s; however the band reformed in 1984 with some subsequent success, which could explain the reference to the band here as part of 1980s culture.

9. B105 is a Top 40 radio station in Queensland.

3 Emotion, Feeling, and Musical Memories

Ahh, Shirley Bassey, that song 'This is My Life' – I can have a damn good cry at that one. Yes, [it's the lyrics] and it's the emotion that she sings. She really sings with her whole heart. Well I find, I find [it] so. It affects me, that one (Bea, age 81).

One of the fundamental aspects of being human is the ability to feel emotion in response to our surroundings and to our own thoughts and memories. Causes of, and reactions to, emotion are encountered in everyday life, typically reaching their greatest heights at momentous occasions or during peak experiences, both positive and negative. Its prevalence in all we do means that along with the visual and aural aspects of our environment, emotion also becomes encoded into memory. In the same vein, emotion is highly implicated with the creation, performance and perception of music. As David Hesmondhalgh points out, "music often feels intensely and emotionally linked to the private self" (2013: 1). Music can make us feel emotion simply due to its beauty or aesthetic, or because of its ability to change our mood, but its emotional meaning can morph and change over time.

Given this, in deconstructing people's musical memory narratives the question of whether all musical memories might be tied to emotion in some way arises. Certainly, many memory narratives that appear here are imbued with an affect of some sort, some in more subtle ways than others. This chapter offers a range of ways of thinking about music, memory and emotion through participants' memory narratives in which emotions are perceived, detailed, expressed or physically felt in relation to music. An in-depth examination of emotionality and its connections within these memories is explored where participants' memories emphasize the plurality of affect within the lifetime soundtrack. Ideas surrounding physical reactions, the use of music at major events and the purposeful use of music to elicit emotional reaction are among the themes guiding the following discussion of the role emotion plays at the intersection of music and memory. Personal stories demonstrate the complexity behind emotional memories, unveiling both commonplace and novel scenarios including romantic relationships, bereavement and loss, and life milestones.

Music, memory and emotion are so closely interrelated in the mind that it is impossible to talk about them without referring to the psychological basis for their connection. Indeed, one of the reasons we think of these three things simultaneously may be because they are processed in the same or adjacent parts of the brain (Janata 2009). Despite philosophical and musicological advances into the ideas of musical expression and emotion, that is, what music itself expresses – if anything (see, for example, Cook 1998), there is little in the way of existing conceptual deliberation on their connection that specifically includes memory as a catalytic agent. The relationship between music and emotion has received much attention through focused exploration in music psychology and neuroscience which spans ideas from the ability for musical structures to express or evoke emotions, to the influence of personality and mood, as well as therapeutic applications (see, for example, Juslin and Sloboda 2010). Certainly, humans are hard-wired to respond to music, beginning with sensory development of the foetus in the womb, where particularly in the third trimester of gestation, the rhythms of the mother's body and elements of her speech filter through to the baby (DeCasper *et al.* 1994). Music is used in many cultures as a method of calming, soothing or entertaining infants and children because of our nature to respond cognitively and emotionally to particular musical patterns, though knowledge of this continues to be learnt over time (Barrett 2009; Rock, Trainor and Addison 1999; Thompson 2015). As we age, music affects the brain in a range of different ways that might provoke emotion, often tied to our developmental progress (e.g. childhood, adolescence, adulthood). Research into the purpose or function of this particular relationship persists, just as arguments on why we as humans make music or include music as part of everyday practices are perpetually developing. There is a tension between the specific subject of much of this work, and the relationship we have at hand in this chapter, which is not concerned with the argument of whether or not music can evoke emotion simply through its existence, or why it does this, or whether or not music produces similar affects for different people. Instead, the connection I wish to discuss is based on emotion that has become associated with music *and* personal experiences, rather than produced purely by music listening.

Music is often thought to enhance atmospheres to the benefit of social or solemn gatherings, but can also function as a companion in solitude, in times of grief or happiness. Some research in emotion and memory indicates that higher levels of emotion in an original experience can result in more vivid memories (Baumgartner 1992). Though the research underlying this book did not measure vividness per se, some memory narratives suggest that everyday memories of music sit alongside those of higher emotional content in the lifetime soundtrack. At the same time, emotional musical memories were sometimes recalled more easily. Of the studies that do look at the interaction of music and emotion in memory, some trends arise particularly in relation to the intensity and type of emotion produced, usually when music is used as the trigger. For example, music associated with youth, which has already been discussed in this book as significant in the lifetime soundtrack, was shown to elicit higher emotional responses than other times in life (Schulkind *et al.* 1999), which perhaps corresponds to the ease and frequency with which childhood memories were recalled by participants. Of relevance to this chapter are findings from Hays and Minichiello (2005) whose empirical work with older people proposes that emotion is the central agent that supports personal meaning in musical memories. It is this aspect in particular that shapes the way this chapter approaches the emotional stories gathered from interview narratives, for it is in these stories that acute meaning is found by their authors, and the coordination of memory, music and emotion plays out in-situ over time.

Conceptualizing affective musical memories

As Ben Anderson describes in his study of in/voluntary remembering, autobiographically salient music "does not act primarily as an object of meaning but becomes a facilitator, or affective catalyser, that enacts the emergence, and therefore affection, of 'a' memory" (2004: 16). This statement highlights a triangulation between music, memory and affect such that music ceases to be essentialized as something from which meaning is drawn, but rather, these three elements assemble together in a fluid relationship. Anderson's comment also suggests that music acts as a conduit for emotion, rather than that emotion being induced from musical elements alone. For my research participants, music acted as a portal to past experiences and associated emotions as Anderson indicates, but further to this, individuals often described certain elements of music as reasons for specific personal engagement with music (see more on this in Chapter 4). With this in mind, I argue that rather than music acting as a more or less hollow facilitator of emotion and memory, it enriches the communication of feeling through the affective elements of melody, harmony, tone, timbre and rhythm, and is therefore a significant agent in a triangulated interdependent relationship.

Some of the boundaries of the music–memory–emotion connection were revealed by participants' stories and thoughts. Though not exhaustive, there are several points of intersection that are worth putting forth. The first exemplifies the aforementioned issues with arguments on the interpretation of emotional substance particularly in pure non-vocal music (*can* music express emotion?): in the mnemonic relationship between music and emotion, affect must be assigned by the listener, but it need not align with any authorized notions of the sort of feelings that music "should" evoke:

> One other thing that they used to do on local radio in those days was they used to broadcast the reading of the funeral notices from the paper. They used to do it three times a day, one in the morning, once around noon and then once early evening … The theme music they used to play to lead up to these was um, a Largo by Handel from *Xerces*. It's not a particularly sad piece of music, it's a beautiful piece of music, but whenever I hear that now it kind of makes me feel sad because it was always associated with people dying, and the funeral notices. In a lot of cases they were people who you knew, or they might have been parents or grandparents of kids you were going to school with and things like that because they were all local people. And even that now still, I hear that, it's a beautiful piece of music, it makes me feel sad (Henry, age 70).

In his reflection, Henry perceives the music as aesthetically "beautiful", but without his mnemonic association he does not feel that the music communicates any particular emotion. Despite this, Henry has associated the work with sadness. It would appear this was invoked from a young age through repeated experience: he did not hear this piece just once, but many times, which likely helped to ingrain the connection to funerals. Perhaps it is also only in retrospect that Henry can differentiate between his objective and subjective responses to the music.

A second point of intersection manifests in the appealing tension in the creation of emotional music memories that sits between familiarity and novelty. On the one hand, repeated experiences of the same sequence of music and context can reinforce feelings so that cumulatively they are perceived as somewhat greater than the sum of their parts, as in Henry's narrative. On the other hand, highly emotional experiences can occur when well-known music is heard in unexpected circumstances, creating sharp edges around vivid memories. An avid metal and hard rock fan, Jeremy described in his interview how a pivotal encounter changed his memory for a particular album:

> I do remember an instance of what I was listening to when I was feeling particularly shitty about how long it was taking me to immigrate [from Canada to Australia to be with his fiancé]. I was skateboarding to work and I had Pantera on my CD player and I had it because it was just a fully aggressive band and I was just, I was starting to feel numb at that point, being in limbo but not doing anything. And I was skateboarding along and obviously wasn't paying attention, hit a rock or crack or something and just flew forward and … tore my hands open and I just [had] an intense burning gravel rash pain on my hands, "oh well, I can feel something now", and I remember Pantera, it was the CD I chose to put on that morning was Pantera (Jeremy, age 36).

In this story, two familiar elements – a Pantera album and travelling to work on a skateboard – are interrupted by a fall. In retrospection, Jeremy has also created a holistic narrative that accounts not only for the sequence of events that day, but the metaphorical significance of the contrast between his emotional funk and a violent plunge to the ground. Unlike Henry's memory, this is ostensibly a one-off event, but it is one that has more specific and unique contexts. The way in which both narratives are told signals their meaning has crystallized with help of time and reflexive thought.

Throughout this chapter, participant narratives will demonstrate that emotion and music can be tied into autobiographical memories in a variety of ways. For some people, the music and emotion are more closely paired, and memories of specific events relating to this feeling are secondary; for others, music is tied directly to memory, with atmospheric feelings and affected states recalled soon after. There appears to be some basic patterns through which music, memory and emotion interact. A useful way to think about how this might occur is to look to the methods used in the empirical study of musical memory. Many psychological studies employ cue methods in which memory or emotion is triggered – often for ease of measurement. When music is used in this way, a clear path between music and potentially simultaneous feeling and memory can be enacted. This is the most scientifically rational, and therefore most frequently used method for understanding how these three elements play out. In contrast to this, most interviews conducted for this research were done in the absence of music, and were led by verbal prompts. As one of the few studies of its kind, where qualitative, narrative data is collected over quantitative, this research reveals another equally rational process of connecting music, memory and emotion. Typically, my interviewees would imagine and verbalize a memory that referred to music and, often, emotion. Additionally, emotion can become caught between music and memory, such that the original source of emotionality becomes disconnected. Vincent expressed such an experience while watching television:

> Only a month, two months ago, on "Hymns of Praise" there was –
> I can't even remember what it was, I can't remember why, but I sat
> there, [my wife] was sitting there, and I have to surreptitiously take
> my glasses off and wipe a little tear away, because it brought some-
> thing back, hearing whatever that was. But it has to play again for
> me to remember what it was – do you understand what I mean? So,
> I'm either a softie or you know, the music was part of the experience
> that opens the door and lets you re-experience it (Vincent, age 77).

Vincent's comment during the interview came after nearly an hour of reflecting upon the importance of music in his life. He was quite aware of music's emotional effect on him in a general sense; however, there is a distinct space between the affect he feels here and the original source. What I am suggesting, then, is that there are several ways that emotion is bound to the interaction between music and memories.

This chapter now turns to instances of emotion's integration into musical memories. Though emotion was present, if not dominant, in a lot of memory narratives, there seemed to be several recurring themes that were common to just about everyone. The strongest affective musical memories often surrounded love and lovers, grief, sadness and ways of coping with or expressing those emotions. Music in these instances is often symbolic, representing ineffable feelings in totality, acting as a touchstone to revisit more subtle, underlying themes of resilience, tribute, and deep personal connections.

Lovers, old and new: Break-up music, and 'our song'

Romantic partners can often greatly influence each other in many ways, including preferences for arts and culture. Music is frequently used as a way of bonding with others, and is also sometimes used to express feelings which may not be as subtly explained in spoken words. The connections made between lovers through music has been widely described in colloquial ways, with the idea of "our song" in popular culture, for example the country hit, 'They're Playing our Song' (released by George Jones and Tammy Wynnette in 1995) or the musical by the same name (composed by Carole Bayer Sager and Marvin Hamlisch in 1978), and the use of the mixtape as a way of relating to one another (as in Nick Hornby's book *High Fidelity*, 1995).

Significant others featured regularly in relayed memory narratives in this research, though associations with past partners were more common than current ones. When used as a basis for creating social bonds, especially in terms of courtship, strong emotions can become tied to specific music that a couple experienced together, or with music that was strongly preferred by only one person in the relationship. Songs that are recognized as having shared significance are particularly rich in their associations: often, these songs don't just represent one moment or a single feeling, but often encapsulate something much broader about the relationship, and can therefore be emotionally complex.

Music that becomes significant in a relationship can be already familiar to people before they enter a relationship – it might feature in their lifetime soundtrack and have some existing associations. In this scenario, the music can become a meeting point or bridge between two soundtracks. This was the case with Mark and Stella, who were interviewed separately yet both told a similar narrative:

> My mum used to play the *Riverdance* soundtrack a lot, so if I ever
> hear that I sort of think about her. And I also think about Stella
> as well because she, when we first started talking to each other we

> were showing each other all music that we liked and then she randomly sent me some *Riverdance* thing and I told her all about how that was in my childhood (Mark, age 22).

> Like when I first met Mark, we would like chat on MSN[1] in the night times, yeah classic MSN conversations, and you could link each other like, files, and so we like shared our favourite music, so some songs I link with him … There's this musical called *Riverdance* … it's probably my favourite CD right, *Riverdance on Broadway* … And I told Mark that, and he was like, you know what I have a live version, and he sent me this – like my favourite song off it, but a live version and I like, lost my shit. But I associate that with him (Stella, age 22).

Both Mark and Stella already held *Riverdance* in their own lifetime soundtrack before they met, and both brought individual perspectives on this music: for example, Mark already associated it with his mother. Through their continued relationship, the song's personal meanings have been broadened to include reference to each other as the song is clearly shared as a mutual musical memory.

First experiences in life are often remembered sharply and can become significant in autobiographical memory (Rubin and Kozin 1984), particularly as "temporal landmarks" (Shum 1998), where they help to structure the way we think about our personal experiences unfolding over time (Conway 1990). Notably, first experiences of love and romantic relationships that often come with a rush of new feelings and uncertainties are particularly well remembered (see Robinson 1992). Paul constructed a dramatic history of what retrospectively became the "break-up music" that accompanied the end of a relationship with his first girlfriend. Sparked from a discussion about travel and transportation, Paul began a story about his strong association between particular music and a past love interest.

> There's an Australian band called The Black Eyed Susans. I got into this band because I loved a girl whose name was Susan who had black eyes [laughter] … and they had an album called *This One Eats Souls* … and I just had broken up with this – my first long-term relationship – and I'd gone to Sydney and she was there but had no money and we were both nuts over each other, and all sorts of crazy things happened. I was staying with my grandparents but going into the city and we were kind of chasing each other round the city being silly, spending time together in hotel rooms when we shouldn't, but I'd be heading to and from those very traumatic engagements with her listening to *This One Eats Souls*. Actually, that particular track (Paul, age 42).

This memory seems chaotic and volatile – Paul uses the word "traumatic" to describe the experience, though this feeling may be something understood only in retrospect. Through practices of reflection, the temporal flow of events can become compressed, especially when one song or artist becomes personally associated with multiple yet similar events. The music can come to represent a period of time though the gathered remnants of the memories remain quite vivid – this is a "cloud memory" as described in Chapter 1. From this story it is also possible to construct parallels of intentionality, and something akin to serendipity; at the time of the event Paul might have selected the music for any number of reasons, including an increasing association with his partner; however, he did not necessarily intend for this music to become the soundtrack to their break-up. Paul concludes the story by recounting how it was only recently that he was reminded of the music and the whole experience, whilst riding a train in Sydney – a contextual feature of this memory. Along with unpleasant experiences, music that becomes associated with unwanted feelings is often evaded, and not sought out. This can sometimes lead to musical memories becoming kept in a sort of *memory vacuum* where details can be forgotten and unexpectedly brought to mind through sensory triggers, including the music itself (see Chapter 4).

When a relationship breaks down for the first time, the intensity of emotion can be high; people frequently seek support, sometimes finding it in music:

> I got dumped by my first big love when I was 22 … there was a song that came out which really clicked … the song was um, how does it go, "I was in love with you but you weren't in love with me"[2] … and basically that was the situation at the time, I was in love with him and he wasn't in love with me, and I remember sitting in the … middle of the lounge room floor listening to this song, drinking a six-pack [of beer] and crying (Susan, age 52).

Fatefully, a newly released song that expressed just what Susan was feeling became available to her at the right time. The inclusion of space and place paints a picture of the narrator in solitude, indulging her emotion through the relatability of the song. Listening to music after a break-up can become ritualistic: a coping mechanism for excessive emotion which Emmers and Hart (1996) explain may be self-destructive, categorizing it alongside behaviours such as crying, drinking and eating to excess, and smoking. In other instances, participants may not have been seeking out empathetic music but simply by virtue of its manifestation at a certain time, it became tangled into autobiographical memory. Angela described such an instance when she said:

> When I relate to the first movie I saw after I broke up with my hus-
> band [which] was *Love Actually* and there's that whole Joni Mitch-
> ell song what's it called, can't think of the name of it, but it's just
> really depressing and it was just like, just brings – I mean I love it
> now to listen to it, but if I listen to it I'm feeling a bit sad because it
> brings back that memory ... something about her and the way she
> sings and the words she uses (Angela, age 43).

It was later revealed the song Angela associates with her marriage break-
up is 'River' (1971). The situation described by Angela may be a product of
an affected state, something noted by Knobloch and Zillmann (2003) who
describe the vulnerabilities of listening to "love-lamenting" tunes after a relationship break-up. Like others, Angela finds something relatable to her specific
situation in the lyrics of the song. Importantly, she also refers to the sound of
the song more abstractly, where the vocal timbre and performer aesthetic also
influence the emotion and meaning that are drawn from the music.

In a process similar to the way both Angela and Susan came to engage
with their respective break-up songs, Vivian, below, tells of how she chanced
upon a certain song that she found herself playing repeatedly throughout her
divorce process. Again, this music was not sought out but, rather, it was a
coincidentally popular song that year:

> Yes, well and actually I am divorced ... but I remember at the time,
> I remember there was a Cher song that I used to listen to, and I
> think it was something like that song, I don't know what it was
> called, do you believe in love after life or life after love. Yeah that
> song, and I remember thinking, "Oh god this is a really good song"
> ... I remember my husband saying to me, "God, is this some sort
> of anthem for you?" or something like that, and I thought, "Gee,
> I must be playing it a lot". But I really liked the song and that was
> one song at the time I remember thinking maybe this is relevant. It
> just came out at that time and maybe it was relevant to what I was
> experiencing at the time (Vivian, age 51).

Vivian's recollection suggests that there is some level of absent-mindedness in
suddenly relating to a song that empathizes with the listener's thoughts and
feelings at a point in time: in the stories presented here, people are not always
seeking or choosing songs necessarily, but rather the song seems to emerge
unbidden. In this case the song communicates through its lyrics a sense of
hope that related directly to Vivian's situation. Although she did not fully recognize the reality of why she was relating so strongly to this song in the first
instance, with the passing of time Vivian has come to see her circumstances
expressed in the music. Laura Vroomen (2004) recognized similar behaviour
occurring in her study of female Kate Bush fans. She notes that in identifying

with song lyrics that describe female-centric experiences, participants could maintain feelings of self-worth, drawing on discourses of strength and female empowerment. Vroomen's interviewees connected with various aspects of feminism as they perceived them to exist in Kate Bush's music and persona. Songs such as 'Believe' by Cher, and also 'River' by Joni Mitchell, similarly present feminist elements of the strong, autonomous woman, who has also undergone romantic hardship. Both Vivian's and Angela's connection with their respective songs is founded in a personal resonance with these properties such that the song's message helped them through an emotionally difficult stage. In the previous memory narratives, it is also striking that lyrics were the principal means for participants to recognize and recall the song – the exact title eludes them all. Perhaps this is due to the dominance of the lyrics and the style of singing as communicating empathy, directed in personal ways to the listener.

Funerals, bereavement, grief

Just as music is associated with significant others during life, the same is true of music in times of bereavement. The nature of music to become associated with deceased loved ones can sometimes manifest in the selection of music to be played in their remembrance, especially at their funeral service. Music can have an important role within commemorative service and is common across the funeral rituals of many cultures. In Western cultures, Christian music dominated the funeral service until the late twentieth century and often centred on solemn or grave musical themes (Garrido and Davidson 2016). Funerals in the fieldwork area of south-east Queensland could be said to follow this trend, given the dominance of Christian-based faiths throughout the twentieth century. Certainly, during the last century funeral rites in Australia have generally been performed within the church or other religious setting, aligning with traditional Western frameworks of mourning etiquette. More recently, there has been an increase in the use of secular music alongside hymns (Parsons 2008, cited in Caswell 2012) which also reflects an increased personalization of the traditional funeral service (Howarth 2000; Emke 2002; Holloway *et al.* 2013). Such choices are significant in terms of the lifetime soundtracks of the departed, as well as the soundtracks of those people present at the service.

The dynamic between funeral ceremonies, deceased family or friends, and music varies greatly between individuals. Musical associations with the deceased person are generally made prior to the person passing but may only be realized at the time of bereavement. The connections made between memory and music at this time become strong bonds that can allow us to maintain a link to a loved one who has passed away. As Baraldi (2009: 257) notes, the aesthetic meaning of music is transformed when it is embedded in social action – that is to say, a secular song, for example, that is played at a funeral may just as easily be used at a wedding; however, its meaning is informed by the occasion. Music chosen by individuals prior to their passing is likely to be an expression of their perceived self-identity, whereas music chosen by others may be chosen from, or be a projection onto, the individual's lifetime soundtrack so that it represents that person or the bond they shared in some way.

Music in memory narratives about funeral ceremonies represents the unique bond between people that can be encapsulated in music. At these events of sorrow and loss, music often serves to align the flow of the service, but also to aid emotional expression, at least in many modern Western societies (Adamson and Holloway 2012). In Paul's recollection, it is clear that music's interaction with emotion can be most acute in its use at funeral ceremonies:

> ... someone very close to me, their parent died, and I helped them through the ceremony and all that kind of thing, and I think it was a song called 'You Raise Me Up' or something like that which I imagine is pretty standard funeral fare ... I think the deceased person really loved that song but ... it's not something I would ever listen to in my own life. But in that particular context – because apparently there was a connection between the deceased person and the piece of music – plus the actual moment in the ceremony where it was played it was extremely moving. It was the moment where you know the taps turned on and then everybody cried. Um, but actually the music was contingent in that situation, you know they could have just as easily played 'It Was a Good Year for the Roses' or you know, or certain things that would be aberrant – 'Ding Dong the Witch is Dead' or something wouldn't be appropriate in that moment, but that was quite instructive to me because I thought, you know it was context dependent ... at that particular point after everyone had stopped talking and the casket was being wheeled out, we needed something at that time that would allow us to, you know, cry (Paul, age 42).

In Paul's encounter, the music was used as a signifier that aided the release of emotion collectively. The music itself, as Paul implies, did not need to be meaningful to every person present at the event, and in fact, it did not hold any value to him prior to this experience; however, the intent of the music in the situation was clearly understood. Additionally, the choice of music is reflective of the deceased (Paul says that the person "really loved that song"), and as such it may engage with family or friends' memories of the individual (see also Caswell 2012). Interestingly, Paul here is more of an onlooker, there to support a good friend, but perhaps having little personal connection with the deceased, which raises a question as to why this event might stay within his lifetime soundtrack. At the time of our interview, this experience was quite recent, and in time it may fade as it becomes compared to other more personal encounters through the canonization process. Moreover though, Paul acknowledges the impact of the music as being "instructive" – as per the functions of memory (Chapter 1); this is perhaps closer to the core of why this memory is persisting with him, at least in the short-term.

One of the younger research participants, Will, stated that he rarely connects emotionally with music. Upon questioning his encounters with music at major events, however, Will recounts a moment of unexpected emotion that was triggered by music at his grandfather's funeral:

> I remember just sitting there, everyone is bawling around me like, during the funeral, and I didn't, I was a bit like, "should I be crying?" And then as soon as my sister's [pre-recorded piano] piece came on, that just sent me off ... and that song would set me off again probably, if I heard it again ... I think it was just a random piano piece my sister had [played] but it's that kind of slow 'Moonlight Sonata' kind of style, and my grandad had done this rusty recording [of her performing it], meaning he'd done it with whatever, a tape or something like that. Oh, I definitely have been moved by music (Will, age 26).

Within the interview Will noted that his associations for these significant people in this scenario extend more towards his sister than his grandfather due to her involvement in making the music itself. Nonetheless, the emotion triggered by the music is due to its use in the typically emotional context of a funeral ceremony. As mentioned in some other memory narratives in this book, playback technologies through which music is heard can steep music with a certain aesthetic. In this case it has been incorporated into the emotional and mnemonic connections within Will's lifetime soundtrack. Even though Will describes his connection with music as principally non-emotional, it is compelling to note his admission that this particular moment resonates in such a way that he would feel a similar wave of emotion if he were to hear the music again.

Just as music at funeral ceremonies can be used to aid the expression of emotions associated with bereavement, it can also be used to change the atmosphere of proceedings. In their study of music choice within funerals in the United Kingdom, Adamson and Holloway (2012: 44–45) found that celebrants or religious figures suggested families pace the proceedings with musical interludes, especially in the middle and at the end of ceremonies, to allow mourners time to reflect or pray – something that Paul, above, recognized ("we needed something at that time that would allow us to, you know, cry"). Families interviewed for the study noted especially their choice of music to end the ceremony, which was intended to lighten the mood and have an uplifting effect. This last point was described by a young participant in my study, Amelia, who outlined her first funeral experience:

> Probably the first person, the closest, that died, which is my Nana. And it was just when they played 'Time to Say Goodbye'. I just remember ... none of us could contain ourselves, it was just the saddest moment. But at the same time we felt happy, they played this really nice video that [my aunt] put together ... I don't remember what was playing behind it but it was really daggy music and it was really happy and it just ... lifted the mood completely. Like everyone pretty much had stopped crying by that point and was laughing and, more celebrating rather than mourning (Amelia, age 19).

Here the music signals that the time of mourning is over: the plurality of musical emotion is active in this narrative, demonstrating the interaction between the aesthetic "feel" of the music and the emotional reactions that it is supposed to engender within the context of the ceremony. These associations may well continue for Amelia, such that she connects the music with the more celebratory aspect of the situation.

Bereavement is a particular period of severe grief suffered by those who survive a significant other (Parkes and Prigerson 2013: xiv). O'Callaghan and colleagues note the critical role music can play at this time, stating that while funerals affirm death and validate the deceased's life, there is a more prolonged and serious stage of grief to come (2013: 104). Music can be used to connect with the deceased beyond commemorative services, and can facilitate mood states through purposeful playing, or even evasion (O'Callaghan et al. 2013). The bond between music and loved ones is a tenuous one – the ease with which music can allow memories and their associated emotions to replay in the mind can be at once a link to fond memories but also a stark reminder of sadness and loss. Bea revealed how the strong connection she feels between music and her husband has also confined her listening habits:

> Isn't that terrible, you know I haven't played my tapes since I lost Nelson? I just can't handle that at present. And yet Nelson's been gone 15 months, but I have not played our player since he's gone, because he played it all the time (Bea, age 81).

For Bea, the music she and her husband used to play is the ultimate representation of their bond. Even the technology once used to play this music has been left untouched, because of the memories that it embodies. In an article discussing the ideas of grief and biography, Walter (1996) notes that the process of grief includes the resolution of feelings; these emotional attachments may be stopping an individual from re-establishing themselves as autonomous from deceased loved ones. From the interview with Bea it would appear that she is still working through the grieving process; music that was associated with her late husband continues to create emotions that seem too strong to purposefully re-experience just yet.

The potential for strong musical bonds to be developed between parents or caregivers and children was emphasized in Chapter 2, where the sharing of the adult's preferred music often provides the foundation and jumping-off point for the lifetime soundtracks of young people in their care. In times of grief these musical memories can materialize, intensifying this connection within the relationship. In the below, interview participant Matthew describes the development of the association between a particular song and his mother. Battling with illness for some time, Matthew's mother was being cared for in their home in Indonesia, refusing to see Western physicians. At the time, Matthew had been learning the tune 'Round Midnight' and over a period of time began to associate this song with his mother's passing:

> I started associating it with, you know, with my mother's death because that was like one of the first times she ever asked me – one time I remember her asking me one time to play something for her, she's like "just play me something" you know, and she was on her way out ... you know, I played it and she sort of just went "that's nice" you know, and I was like, "oh, it is nice I guess" ... by that time my Mum was in the ICU, and ... I got there, and she was basically going through a fit of some type, um and I played [a recording of me playing] and she calmed down immediately ... So yeah I sort of associate it, and that was the song that I played at her funeral in the end ... I guess, these days I guess I associate it more with change rather than with my mother's death (Matthew, age 25).

For Matthew, this song has a long history; rather than being associated with one discrete event, Matthew described how the song has come in and out of his life since his mother's passing. Its continued presence in his life potentially contributed to his feeling that the song represents change rather than death or bereavement. Soon after the illness and death of Matthew's mother, his family moved to Australia, which likely further emphasizes the symbolism the tune holds for feelings surrounding change.

In an instance of forethought on the ties between parents, shared music, and feeling, in our interview Anna described how she had already thought about the cultural bonds shared with her father that represented a very firm association. Below she describes her ideas of what it will be like when her father passes away:

> But the concept of like, when Dad dies, The Beatles will make me cry because it's something I associate with him, and it won't nec-

essarily matter the kind of songs I think, just that that's a musical
genre or band that's associated with him. And so [it] doesn't necessarily have to be the content of the music that is emotionally pull-
ing but the associations with it (Anna, age 18).

The participant's rationale for knowing that any of The Beatles' music will
forever be reminiscent of her father resonates with the idea of affect flow-
ing within music. Rather than attributing sadness to the articulation of this
affect in the music itself, Anna believes it is the associations she has with the
music that will have emotional impact. It also highlights again the bonding
between parent and child that can be signified through shared soundtracks,
which is exacerbated in times of bereavement. The kinds of physical reactions
people have in relation to the complex feelings that come with grief can also
affect listeners more broadly for a range of reasons. Though some instances
of physical reactions have hereto been implied, the following section looks
more closely at the ways in which the body sometimes responds to emotional
music memories.

Corporeal reactions: The affective power of musical memories

The range of responses people may have to music has been relatively well-
documented, from mental reactions, with which much of this book is concerned, to physical reactions, which can be both obvious and invisible.
Sensations like goose bumps and shivers can accompany music listening in a
range of contexts (Nusbaum *et al.* 2014) – as can the thought or act of weeping. Some arguments in music psychology outline a concept of musical expectations – where the manipulation of rhythm, harmony, melody or timbre can
align with or challenge the listener's anticipation of what will happen next
(e.g. Huron 2006), inducing emotions and physical reactions. Stengs (2018)
argues that physical sensations and emotion can be separated, and moreover that these two things are only aligned when people try to make sense of
their physical responses by assigning them an emotion. In terms of musical
memory, emotions experienced when memories are recalled are similar to
those present in the original experience (Janata *et al.* 2007; Cady *et al.* 2008),
which helps to consolidate meaning within the lifetime soundtrack. The outward expression of emotion was one of the first aspects of emotional connection to music or memory mentioned by participants.

The most common recollection and in-situ reaction for people in this
research was that of weeping. For some, this reaction had occurred at the
time of the event in question, and for others, the affective expression was
triggered within our interview at the thought of the music and personal associations thereof. The prevalence of weeping when listening to music has been
described by Gabrielsson, whose long-term project probing the public on

strong experiences with music resulted in nearly a quarter of his participants (the total numbering nearly one thousand) including the physical reaction of tears in their accounts (2011: 374). Weeping can serve the purpose of "coping with emotional states that seem intolerable" (Lipe 1980: 27), though crying may express joy as much as it expresses sadness (Barbalet 2005: 138). In reaction to music in particular, Cotter *et al.* (2018a) found two main experiences are typical of aesthetic crying, described either as *in awe* or *in sadness*. With extensive analysis, they identified features of music that were common to each kind of experience, such as genre, complexity, live or recorded music, subjective qualities and listening environment. Particularly relevant to the context of this research was the finding that sad experiences were more likely when the music was familiar or personally meaningful, and reminded them of someone they knew (Cotter *et al.* 2018b: 13). Awe-inspired music on the other hand was often complex and beautiful, with such feelings more likely to be experienced in the company of others; however, these characteristics suggest a diminished association with autobiographical memory than sad crying experiences. Participants in my research were not asked specifically about music that made them cry or think about crying, but both thoughts and actions thereof occasionally occurred spontaneously within interviews. Described below, these narratives could arguably be reduced to the categories of "awe" or "sadness"; however, such labels seem somewhat too simplistic compared to the depth of emotion that is articulated.

The below narrative from Tony describes a joyous kind of weeping as an expression of sudden gladness – something akin to Cotter and colleagues' affect of awe. In this scenario, Tony is getting back together with some of his old band mates, sometime after they had gone their separate ways:

> So maybe 10 or 15 years ago I was contacted by ... one of the writers of ['Little Ray of Sunshine'] and ... he asked me if I'd be available to do some gigs with him, so I joined his backing band. And the first night that we played was at Southport RSL. And when it got to 'Little Ray of Sunshine', I found myself tearing up, because subsequently I'd had a baby daughter, she's 20 now, so she would have been about four or five at the time, so my emotional reaction to that [was] completely out – the rehearsal was fine, it was just doing the song you know, same old same old, nothing new here, nothing to look at here let's move on – but when we actually were performing it, it completely resonated with me as a father of a young girl, and I had tears streaming down my face, complete emotional venting on stage ... But you forget, I mean there's a song I would have played at least hundreds if not thousands of times without any kind of emotional impact on me whatsoever, and because my circumstances had changed, and it had been a long gap so it had a chance to slowly morph into

> something meaningful, the meaning just sort of descended on me in a torrent, um and it was one of the most joyous experiences of my playing life that I can recall (Tony, age 62).

Tony's previous experience with this song is significant in realizing the gravity of musical affect: the music is familiar to Tony, and as a musician he has performed this song many times: the patterns of the song are firmly set in his memory. And yet, a number of circumstances aligned on this particular occasion to allow this music to evoke a new kind of meaning. This recollection illuminates not only the strength with which music can draw out emotion, but also how the passage of time can often create a deeper meaning between known music and memories that may not yet be associated with this music. Tony's perception of his young daughter became crystallized during this performance, which as he notes, would not have been possible when he had originally played on the recording of this song.

Music has the affective power to overwhelm, whether through aesthetic means alone or in combination with associated personal meaning. It was striking, however, to hear the mention of bagpipes and bagpipe music in two separate interviews within the relatively small pool of interviewees. Even the thought of such music brings Angela to the brink of tears:

> And probably the worst thing [is] ANZAC Day. I cannot handle it when bagpipes are playing 'Amazing Grace'. That just, oh I tear up just thinking about it, I can't even sit there and look at them walking because it just upsets me so much ... it's just the knowing that they went off to war and a lot of them didn't come back (Angela, age 43).

Angela explains that even though she has no immediate family members who were involved in war, the sentiment of the day, and the reflection upon the loss incurred by many families evokes a consistently emotional episode for her. This raises the question of sadness versus awe in this experience – perhaps here there is an element of both, where Angela is rather in awe of great tragedy, the knowledge of which is stimulated by the music. Vivian is similarly affected by the sound of bagpipes:

> I tell you what really makes me cry almost every time, are the bagpipes, yeah I think so, that must be a history thing, a Scottish, it's almost like a proud thing. I don't necessarily listen to a song and burst into tears, but if you put the bagpipes in front of me inevitably every time I'll tear up. So I think that's like a ... could be just the sentimental or – because when you think about it they're a bloody awful sounding instrument, there's nothing nice about them – but yeah it's just that feeling that I get from bagpipes (Vivian, age 51).

While Vivian identifies that the sound of bagpipes moves her emotionally, she also supposes this might be related to her Scottish heritage. What is most likely occurring here, rather than feelings of awe or sadness, is a product of association, and a notion of patriotism. Research into the use of bagpipes for recruitment to the British Army in the First World War shows that use of the Scottish bagpipes became part of the propaganda as a symbol of cultural identity: the sight of national dress (e.g. kilts) and the sound of bagpipes were employed to rouse a sense of nationalism that would drive men to enlist (Shansky 2014). Given that Vivian notes that she spent part of her childhood in Scotland, it is possible that she associates the sound of bagpipes with autobiographical memories of this time, and by extension this evokes a sense of patriotism and pride in her family origin.

In some instances, the recollection of strong emotion resulted in the interviewee tearing up as they described their memories. Such displays signal music does not necessarily need to be playing to evoke a memory or an emotional reaction. The story below emerged while Paul was recounting childhood memories:

> I remember once quite vividly being in bed – and we quite liked the song and there were other songs on the cassette that we quite liked – an album called *Fate for Breakfast* [by Art Garfunkel] um, but yeah my father once, [he] wasn't a very emotionally expressive man at all, I was lying in bed and he came in and he told me that when he hears 'Bright Eyes' he thinks of me (Paul, age 42).

This memory is clearly special to Paul, who mentioned Simon and Garfunkel and their respective solo music to be part of his own lifetime soundtrack. Paul paused as he thought a little more while tears welled in his eyes, before moving on to other memories. This memory involves reflecting not only on childhood, but also on a connection with a parental figure. While this occurred in most interviews when people described music in their childhood, just a handful were moved to tears.

Another person to whom this happened was Ian (age 60), who had a playlist on hand during the interview that he had compiled for his recent sixtieth birthday party. He described the playlist as containing a great deal of songs that were significant to him and represented different eras of his life. In this interview, we sat beside his computer and played songs from the playlist in a rough chronological order, while Ian noted how each song reminded him of an event, person, or geographical space he had experienced in his life. During this process, Ian became tearful at a number of points. The first song Ian played – 'Mambo Italiano' (the Dean Martin version) – he described as "Mum's song", then going on to talk about her fondly, he became tearful. Another twenty minutes on and Ian selects 'Georgia on My Mind' by Ray

Charles: "I used to really like Ray Charles. This was different. This is beautiful." I begin to ask him if it reminds him of anything special, and there is a long pause – Ian is getting very emotional about the music, and obviously does not want to speak further about it. He switches to the next song, and pushes ahead with a different topic.

Another example comes from Bea, mentioned several times in this chapter, who was teary a few times throughout her interview. When speaking about songs that are particularly special to her, she recounts the loss of her husband, and her son, both of which occurred in the years preceding our conversation. She connects music with them that was played at their funerals, and also songs that were their favourites. She described how music helps get her through her day:

> The song I do sing a lot to myself [pause, Bea dabs at her eyes with her handkerchief] isn't it terrible, I'll be right in a minute [pause]. One of them is 'Over the Rainbow' and um, I get a bit emotional with that. And ah, 'One Day He'll Come Along, The Man I Love'. So I don't know, people might think I'm a bit funny, but I'll lay there and just have a little sing to myself (Bea, age 81).

Bea now lives alone and finds that listening to the radio and singing to herself helps her express her feelings and thoughts. The music provides a connection to her loved ones that she can access at any time through singing. As depicted earlier in this chapter, Bea avoids the cassette tapes that remind her of her husband, but with her musical background she allows herself to re-experience music in her own way. Certainly, Bea's story is one of direct connection with loved ones and memories that evoke the saddening experience of crying. Emotional reactions to music are not uncommon, but they can be deeply personal. In describing the ways this kind of reaction played out for some participants, it is possible to see that there is a sort of rawness that can be caused and reopened by music and affiliated memories. Though they may lie dormant, these narratives describe almost tangible portals not only into time, but also into complex and sometimes inexplicable emotion.

Reflexive use of affective musical memories

When an awareness of the affective power of music becomes developed, we sometimes actively avoid or indulge in music to cause, or relieve, particular feelings by revisiting music that has stimulated or satisfied in the past. As one of the more obvious curiosities in the psychology of music, there has been a swathe of research demonstrating the effects of music to enhance or mitigate mood and emotive states (e.g. Hargreaves and North 1999; DeNora 2000; Sloboda 2005). In similar ways to the instances of "break-up music" or funeral selections, there are also times when music is used purposefully, for activities of emotional reflection. A good deal of research in psychology and neuroscience looks into the issues surrounding the deliberate use of music, especially when feeling sad, as a way of affirming emotion, and even feeling pleasure, but sometimes also prolonging potentially negative feelings by reliving the associated memories (e.g. Sachs, Damasio and Habibi 2015; van den Tol and Edwards 2013, 2015). For example, in a study that contrasted musical choices of individuals with depression with those without depression, Wilhelm, Gillis, Schubert and Whittle (2013) found that while mentally healthy people chose music for stimulation, motivation and energy, those who were depressed tended to select music to express or reflect their emotive state. This can create a complicated relationship between the listener, the music, and the situations and circumstances which become represented within the lifetime soundtrack.

One respondent, Susan, went into great detail about music she had trouble listening to due to its associations with people in her past. Some years ago, Susan's marriage was breaking down. It was a tumultuous time for her, as she went through phases of weight-loss and emotional confusion over the state of her relationship with her husband. She described how certain music became caught up with the memories and emotion of that time:

> *Susan*: I would actually like to undo a memory that I have with a certain album ... 'Cause I love the album, but I played it a lot when my marriage was breaking up. And now when I play it I feel so horrible and sad inside that I um, I'd like to get rid of that, I'd like to undo that connection 'cause I really love it. It's the Foo Fighters album, they made it in honour of [Kurt Cobain]. Now Grohl and he were close, they were close friends and, he made this album, even one of the songs is called 'In Your Honour' and it's actually a double album, one CD is full of heavy, 'cause Foo Fighters is heavy, but the other one's all ballads. And I used to play the ballad one because I loved it, I discovered it around that era ... and I used to listen to it to try and relax but at the same time now it's caught up with that pain, and sadness, so um, I'd love to be able to undo that ... I might work on it 'cause I just love it.

> *Interviewer*: Do you avoid putting it on?

> *Susan*: Yes. Umm but maybe I should so I can, I don't know, see some schools of thought say that you've gotta go through it to release it and other people say you don't have to go through all that pain, you can just do something and release it (Susan, age 52).

Susan still wants to listen to the album, even though she knows it may trigger a range of possibly unpleasant feelings associated with this experience – she feels torn between her aesthetic enjoyment of the album and her mnemonic associations.

During this time Susan engaged in what she called an emotional extra-marital affair, in which she became infatuated with a co-worker. In terminating that relationship while her marriage was still breaking down, Susan describes how she often used to listen to, or was exposed to music. Subsequently, this music has become strongly entangled in her memories and emotions from that time:

> One song particularly through that era … around the time our marriage was breaking down, I got a crush on somebody at work and that crush was just an emotional affair … And had this enormous sadness oh and feeling, well I can't do anything about it, and then having this emotional affair I had this huge amount of guilt … So around that era I watched the movie *The Closer* … And the song … in that movie is 'The Blower's Daughter' by Damien Rice. That song can reduce, did reduce me to sobs, it is just so poignant, and, and specific to what was going on at the time, that it, I remember, playing it over and over again. If you've got a bruise you push it. And I played it and I would be bawling my eyes out (Susan, age 52).

Here Susan describes purposefully playing music that fuelled her emotional state, acknowledging the aspect of ego, and the implication of self-assessment to the situation. Being able to recognize and accept emotions through their articulation in a song meant that Susan was able to reflect on her situation in a way that is both focused and emotionally crushing. The music mentioned in her narratives comprises a therapeutic element such that Susan used the music to reflect upon her experience and validate her emotional state. This self-administered treatment enables a process of emotional and mental healing; while Susan may not have been consciously aware of this element, her desire to repeatedly listen to the music is potentially driven by a need to process her feelings in various ways. This is similar to the connection that another participant, Vivian, formed with a Cher song (see above); however, while Vivian related to music in a positive way, Susan is further endorsing her negative feelings by purposefully playing the music. By playing and replaying the music, she was able to come to understand her emotions and also attain a form of empathy from the music.

Susan's tale illustrates the use of music to indulge or satisfy an emotion, but this is just one way in which people can use music reflexively. Paul tells of music to which he now habitually returns because of its effect on his mood:

> I remember after some, you know, dreadful argument with my partner, going for a drive and ... feeling so angry that I could have crashed the car or if I was a different kind of person, got hammered drunk or done something like that. But instead, played this particular piece of music on the car stereo that I found soothing, and [it] was almost like being talked down by a sort of hostage negotiator. It felt like a very skilled piece of meditation that was being brought upon me. It was a song called 'Weightlifting' by the Trashcan Sinatras and the chorus goes "you will feel a great weight lifting" and I, you know, I've used that song as a balm or a salve in my life, you know I'm feeling bloody terrible I'm going to put that song on. And I still don't really know what the song means, um, but I'm going to listen to that and it's going to lift me out of my emotional funk (Paul, age 42).

Paul notes that the meaning of the song isn't clear to him, yet his description, rich in detail and expressed with a sort of thankful affection, signifies the music has played an important role over many years, mostly as he says, in talking him out of an emotional state. Perhaps adding weight to this feeling is the successful application of music to a situation – "applying" being the operative notion Paul describes in playing the music. The use of music in this way aligns with the idea of a "memory directive", as described by Alea and Bluck (2003) and Pillemer (1998, 2001) where events are vividly remembered in order to guide future thoughts and actions. Despite being borne from an unpleasant event, this memory has become important in guiding how Paul manages his emotion.

A purposeful application of music was also described by some participants in the form of cravings or habits. The use of music in routine ways creates a structure that, when absent, can leave a marked hole in our rituals and routines (DeNora 2000). In the following narrative, Jeremy describes his emotional need for certain music:

> A lot of the music that I get more enjoyment out of isn't [enjoyed by] a lot of people that are my close friends and [my wife] and people, they just don't like it, so it's probably not appropriate for me to play it all the time around other people. But I get a craving for aggressive music and I actually feel more relaxed once I actually get to listen to it. I think that's the biggest emotional connection I have, is if I'm not getting the music that I like, it's like a craving ... I feel sometimes that I have to come home and I have to put on something that I'm gonna really enjoy because a lot of the people that surround me aren't into the same sort of music (Jeremy, age 36).

Jeremy sees his favourite music as a comfort that he feels he can only be allowed to enjoy occasionally. In some ways, his experience of it as an occasional interlude in his life validates his preference for music that is typically unacceptable in his social circles, with the drip-feed of musical encounters only fuelling the craving. Jeremy describes this craving as his only emotional connection with music: his desire to listen to heavy music is likely based within his memories of the way that music has made him feel, or the past experiences that the music accompanies.

In a similar way, Ron also identifies with the need to be satiated by his favourite music:

> It can be anytime of the day or night I'll put on a record because I want to hear that. I haven't heard it for a while. Basically it's a time thing. It's like, starving to death, I've gotta eat, and so I get to a stage where [if] I haven't listened to my sort of music for a long time I've gotta go and do it (Ron, age 59).

Ron refers to the temporal measures that allow or disallow him access to music, similar to the way in which Jeremy describes his ability to only hear his favoured music in certain time intervals. The language used by both participants to describe their need for listening is comparable to basic human needs, such as eating and sleeping. They portray their desire as something like a "need" on which their survival depends, and in some ways, perhaps they are correct. With purposeful listening, individuals may gain aesthetic or spiritual fulfilment which is mediated by reflexive memory practices. Neither Jeremy nor Ron claimed to have any great emotional connection with music in their interviews; however, this need for music that they express suggests a more nuanced way of being affected by music, such that the memory of engaging with certain music provides the rationale for re-experiencing it as often as possible.

Conclusion

Emotion has been shown in this chapter to be integral to much of the personalized musical memories encased in the lifetime soundtrack. Music so easily affects us, that even feelings of irritation or boredom can be embodied in musical memories. This chapter conceptualizes the affective dimension of musical memories as something that enriches that capacity of music to communicate and our ability to perceive music in certain ways, rather than merely acting as a barrier through which music passes. Rather, emotion plays a significant role in colouring the relationship between memory and music, allowing the recognition of original feelings and the creation of renewed perspectives. Musical memories can become representative of highly emotional situations, particularly where music has been the connection (or differential) between individuals, or collective groups. However, affective responses to music can also develop without the need for external influences: practices of reflecting and projecting one's memory with music serves the purpose of consolidating personal feelings but can also create new ones.

This chapter has demonstrated the strength of ties between music and identity, especially in times of mourning. A cumulative personal identity can sometimes be expressed through the pre-selection of music for one's own, or a loved one's funeral service. This scenario creates a particularly special element of the lifetime soundtrack, where music that is personally significant to one person is destined to become a part of the lifetime soundtrack of those in attendance. An investment in music was also revealed by the degree to which participants discussed music, in the sense that for some people, music was something that became very easily personalized and associated with the emotions of significant autobiographical experiences. In some instances, this manifests in bodily reactions; though crying was the main response described in memory narratives, other sensations, like goose bumps, or movements such as nodding or tapping, illustrate a close corporeal relationship with music and emotion. Of note is the great array of other emotional associations that can be found between music and memory, which are not able to be covered here. Their absence calls attention to the complexity with which affect can occupy the spaces between culture and everyday life.

Notes

1. An instant messenger service.
2. Refers to 'You Weren't in Love with Me' by Billy Field, 1981.

4 Recorded Music and Memory: Capturing, Indexing and Archiving the Past

Though the perception of music and its persistence in memory can be explained mechanically as a result of cerebral processing, this does not necessarily account for the ways in which meaning is shared between memory and music. Similarly, in the wider literature on musical memory there is little theorization of how music might so effectively capture personal experiences as they are turned into autobiographical memories. In this chapter, the connection between elements of recorded music, memory and the lifetime soundtrack are conceptualized with reference to ideas of the archive, the fallibility of memory and the infinite reproduction of music via recording and playback technologies. The focus here falls to recorded music, as opposed to live music, due to the ability of recorded music to be played and replayed. Live music, on the other hand, provides quite different, one-off experiences that – while they can be significant in personal memory and contribute to the lifetime soundtrack – cannot be conceptualized in quite the same way as recorded music. The conceptual basis for this chapter rests on two key ideas: the first is that the elements of music and music experience may help to capture the minutiae of experience via the very subjective nature of their existence, and the perception of these elements to the listener. The second refers to the variance between recorded music as a more or less faithful recording that can be repeated, and the fallibility of the autobiographical memory, which can fade and warp over time. This chapter will explore how daily interactions with music can affect the way in which it is associated with memories, and how distinct elements of sound, lyrics, movement and technology can play an important role in musical memory creation and reflection. Through the strength of these elements, the lifetime soundtrack is likened to an archive, or vault, for personal memory.

Archive as memory, memory as archive

To conceptualize the relationship between memory and elements of music experience within this chapter, the idea of the "archive" is applied to both components. In a literal sense, an archive refers to a place, physical or digital, where documents and records are stored (Featherstone 2006). The concept has also been commonly used as a metaphor for memory within many disciplines (Brockmeier 2010), such that memory comprises a proverbial storehouse of information, especially that which is biographical. However, the link between archives and memory has a long history that has been challenged in recent times. Pierre Nora (1989) popularized his concept of *lieux de memoire* (memory places, or sites of memory) in his work, both linking and delineating concepts of memory and history. In so doing, he articulates the historic relationship between memory and the archive:

> Modern memory is, above all, archival. It relies entirely on the materiality of the trace, the immediacy of the recording, the visibility of the image ... hence the obsession with the archive that marks our age, attempting at once the complete conservation of the present as well as the total preservation of the past (1989: 13).

Nora problematizes the role of memory and its perceived function as purely a repository for experience, stating that it is now rather the task of memory to record (an active stance), and the responsibility of the archive to remember (a more passive action). Furthermore, Nora proposes the concept of *lieux de memoire* as archives that can be material, symbolic and functional (1989: 18) as well as malleable, overriding the conceptualization of archives as existing only as physical places:

> For if we accept that the most fundamental purpose of the *lieu de memoire* is to stop time, to block the work of forgetting ... to materialize the immaterial ... all of this in order to capture a maximum of meaning in the fewest signs, it is also clear the *lieux de memoire* only exist because of their capacity for metamorphosis, an endless recycling of their meaning and an unpredictable proliferation of their ramifications (1989: 19).

Created, Nora says, by the interaction of memory and history, *lieux de memoire* refers broadly to sites of collective memory, a complex topic in its own right. But what if we were to consider what personal *lieux de memoire* might entail? In the context of musical memories and the lifetime soundtrack, it is possible that we could think of music, either in singular (song) or collective (album, artist, group) forms, as personal memory places – sites that help to capture memory, but also the mnemonic imagination (as per Keightley and Pickering 2012).

Before expanding on this thought, we ought to consider concurrent developments in memory studies, particularly the "memory crisis" beginning around the same time as Nora's writing in the 1990s. Brockmeier (2010) explains this as a critical challenge to the traditional notion of the memory as an archive, a permanent storehouse for personal and collective histories, through advances in the psychological, social and cultural study of memory. These new ideas diversified the ways in which we can understand memory as being created, re-storied, and drawn upon, but most importantly, they unveiled the failures of memory to retain information, to remain unbiased or without influence from others, or to recall information accurately over long periods of time. Psychologists such as Schacter (2001) and Loftus (1975, 2005) helped to establish that autobiographical memory is easily influenced by others and does not necessarily remain consistent over time. Each time memories are recalled, they are reconstructed in line with the current self, distorting slightly with the addition or subtraction of details, the haze of aging, or a loss of significance (Pillemer 1998). The new perspectives afforded memory by increasing age and experience affect the way we reflect on personal memories – though the core story or feeling may remain constant, the details are affected by acts and practices of remembering (see Chapter 1). So, unlike music, we cannot trust that memories are replicable without loss in fidelity. As such, the terms on which we can compare human memory and traditional ideas of the archive become both narrowed and blurred. Taken together, these theories suggest that autobiographical memory itself does not serve effectively as an archive, though there are some notable similarities. In order to enact something as intangible as memory as some sort of archive, theoretical infrastructure is required. To this end, I propose that the musical contents of the lifetime soundtrack acting as personal *lieux de memoire*, can stand in for an *index* which appoints and accrues meaning from autobiographical experiences, as outlined by DeNora (2000: 67).

What I propose in this chapter is a framework that describes the elements of music and music experience as catalysts for the music-memory relationship. By looking more closely at how participants' memories interact with music, I argue that these elements are the reservoirs for memory – they are the shelves within the archive, the *lieux de memoire*. The action of capturing memory in these elements is critical for the formation of the lifetime soundtrack: the biographical resonances which one feels between music and real-life experience rely on the veritable index to be realized before they can be stored in the canon of the lifetime soundtrack. However, there is more to this relationship than the materialization of a mnemonic index. In their extensive work on the mnemonic imagination, music and photographs, Keightley and Pickering compare elements of their subjects, stating that the physical texts of memory "seem less fallible than human memory, with its inevitable vicissitudes, lacunae and repressions" (2006: 160–61). Among the narratives collected here, it is notable that where music is recorded and accessible in modern listening formats, people accessed their memories via careful selection of music for listening. The ability to do this relies on the music to follow the same course as it always has – the expectations of each verse, chorus, variation or repetition in melody and so on remain the same – the music can be re-experienced with the knowledge that it will sound as it did once before (DeNora 2000). Notwithstanding circumstantial stretching of tape or re-tempering of recordings,[1] one of the most commercialized/marketable properties of recorded music is that it can be played repeatedly with, ostensibly, no loss in fidelity.

Hence, I further propose that memory and music have contrasting capacities to record and replay, and that it is the juxtaposition of these qualities that so readily enables elements of music to capture our personal memories. In other words, memory, which has a weakened ability to accurately recall memories over time, leans into a medium such as music, whose properties of melody, harmony, timbre, and so on can be replicated – ostensibly *ad infinitum*. This is a medium of strength to which the memory system, in need of external support for recall, is drawn. Concurrently, I propose that paramusical elements of musical engagement, such as sound environments and movement (dance) can affect the integration of music and memory. This chapter will explore the idea that elements within and external to music itself facilitate the ability for music to act as an effective archive for the details of space, time and affect that constitute autobiographical memory. There are, of course, variations to this relationship – this chapter will outline the ways our experience with music, technology, and the elements within music itself, can shape the way we relate to music, and by extension, how some music finds its way into the lifetime soundtrack.

Listening for lyrics

The poetic stanzas typical of verse/chorus song form arguably comprise music's most forthright element of communication. Lyrics are of course not present in all styles of music; despite this they may present a particular significance in the meaning of music to individuals and can further embed music and musical experiences into autobiographical memory. The subject of lyrics can resonate with personal experiences and emotions, and can, for some people, express what might seem inexpressible. As documented by DeNora (2000), at times when we do not have words as subtle or appropriate as needed, music – and moreover, the lyrical message within – is sometimes the most effective substitute. This idea, Frith (1987) has previously argued, rationalizes the pre-occupation of popular music with love and romance – the music and lyrics enables complicated emotions to be articulated with greater ease than in regular conversation (see also Horton 1990). The seemingly personal resonance of song lyrics is somewhat at odds with the nature of song writing, and the (ostensible) dissemination of published music to many. The fact that many people may interpret music in the same way, linked to personal experiences, still does not detract from the fact that this mechanism can be used as a tool for meaning-making within the lifetime soundtrack. Lyrics may not only play a role in shaping the soundtrack but can come to represent overarching narratives within the life story, crystallizing as time passes.

Despite the sometimes obvious or seemingly frivolous nature of some song lyrics, which can be at once direct (the vocalist is singing only to you, the sole listener) and broadly relevant, they present an opportunity for meaning-making of the most personal kind. Whereas a riff or melodic theme can be argued to signify a great range of things, lyrics, while still questionable in their meaning, have a narrowed potential due to their likely form in an understandable language. Lyrics can therefore offer a pre-prepared narrative that may align in some ways with aspects of listeners' personal experience or self-identity. For example, the work of Shirley Bassey features heavily in Angela's lifetime soundtrack because of the way her lyrics and persona resonate with Angela's emotional needs:

> Whenever I need to get motivated or if I'm feeling sad [I play] Shirley Bassey – because that was the music I listened to when my ex-husband left, you know all the "I tell myself da da da da!", that really sort of angry, strong, pull yourself together and just get on with it ... I just love Shirley Bassey and I play her CD incessantly (Angela, age 43).

The music of Shirley Bassey became significant for Angela at the time of her marriage break-up and has remained a touchstone for her since. The strong, empowered figure represented by the performance persona of Shirley Bassey, coupled with song lyrics, is drawn upon to provide emotional fortification. Angela later describes her return to this music for the same purposes, but also for celebration. The lyrics that Angela speaks of do not necessarily reflect her autobiographical circumstances in explicit ways, but rather, they resonate more broadly as an expression of her life experiences in a way that allows her to revisit this music for a range of reasons. Interestingly, Shirley Bassey was mentioned as significant for another participant, Bea (age 81), who was quoted in Chapter 3. Bea recalls strong emotions when she hears 'This is My Life' and empathizes with the feminine strength represented by the singer. In specific reference to lyrics, Bea says:

> I've got a couple of songs especially old Satchmo with 'It's A Wonderful World',[2] yes I can get very emotional on that. Because I think it's a very true, true song, I love the words on it, and I think um, it depicts my life ... I think the words in it where you greet people and you smile, that's – yes, so that I would say was my favourite, um, my favourite song (Bea, age 81).

In speaking about this music, Bea became emotional: though she says this song is autobiographical for her, it also connects her to her past, especially people who have passed away. The lyrics have a resonance that relates broadly to life experiences for many people, which Bea responds to as summarizing parts of her personal life story.

As part of a much longer narrative about her marriage break-up and surrounding contexts, Susan (also in Chapter 3 and Chapter 6) described how the song 'Blower's Daughter' by Damien Rice, and the album *Food in the Belly* by Xavier Rudd, became emblematic of this period of her life because of the eerily similar description of her situation within the lyrics of these artists. She tells of listening to the songs repeatedly despite the harrowing emotion she experienced each time. I attempted to find out what it was about the music that made Susan want to continue listening:

> *Interviewer*: Did you take comfort in that music at all, Damien Rice and Xavier Rudd, was it music that … reflected how you felt, was it comforting in any way?
>
> *Susan*: It was more than that, it was, it was you know somebody says, you know, a mind fuck? It was, it was just like a total flip – it was a total, wow! There it is! Um, like, you can't believe that it can be put into that song, and that, total mind fuck, I s'pose. Not only [that], but it's really unusual for it to hit so many levels … but I think it actually hit that soul part (Susan, age 52).

Lyrically and aesthetically the music appeared to describe Susan in deeply personal ways. Her perception of this led her to examine the music repeatedly, and to indulge in the feeling that her situation could be so accurately explained through music. The lyrics specifically have attracted Susan's thoughts, and in essence they have archived this part of her life in great detail. Despite the negative associations with this music, it firmly remains a part of Susan's lifetime soundtrack.

Music can play a key role in how people develop and express their personal identity, especially in their youth (Hargreaves and North 1999; Bennett 2000). Lyrics have the power to influence attitudes or ways of thinking about greater discourses that run through our lives, and can therefore play a role in shaping personal identity and social attitudes, and finding our place in the world:

> Identity is not a thing but a process – an experiential process which is most vividly grasped as music. Music seems to be a key to identity because it offers, so intensely, a sense of both self and others, of the subjective in the collective (Frith 1996: 110).

Frith describes the aptness of music in allowing us to both belong yet feel at once empowered and individual. His thoughts here play into van Dijck's claim (2006) that musical memories sit between the individual and the collective, suggesting that the opportunity for identity refinement is a primary agent in this effect. While identity may become more linked to the greater subcultures to which music belongs, lyrics can present one of the first ways people might attempt to access this culture, to try it on for size. Although we are not always listening for messages amongst song lyrics, their influence may be recognized in retrospect, as Jeremy explains:

> When I was a teenager and in I s'pose early 20s it was a lot to do with lyrics and messages, that's what really, really appealed to me about punk rock was most of the people playing the music were suburban kids my age. And ... their lyrics had to do with sort of what was going [on] in my life ... and some of them got a bit more political. I ... think music had a lot to do, that sort of music, had a lot to do with shaping ... what I thought were good values as well (Jeremy, age 36).

Jeremy's connection to lyrics takes him beyond direct autobiographical similarities to think about politics and community. Jeremy stated he no longer reads as much into lyrics as he once did, indicating a change in how he understands music currently versus the practices of his youth (see also Frith 1987; Bennett 2013). The above excerpts demonstrate just some of the ways in which lyrics can have autobiographical resonance, allowing the lyrics to act as veritable placeholders for past selves or past ways of thinking. Often it seems that the significance of music is not always felt at the time it is experienced. Rather, it is in retrospect, where memories and musical experiences can be compared to one another, that the true meaning of musical memories can be established and maintained within the lifetime soundtrack.

Connecting with sound: Timbre and texture

> *Interviewer*: What is it about music that you enjoy or relate to the most?

> *Lisa*: It's not the lyrics. My ex-boyfriend actually, he was the opposite, he'd just listen to the lyrics and he could sing any song, but I'll listen to a song, 50 times, and sometimes I still won't know the lyrics ... maybe it's the tune that I really like or whatever takes me ... it's funny how some songs, you know strike you ... some songs must – even though I love music I've got no idea about the theory side of it or anything like that so I don't know what to call it. But it sort of goes up and down, I don't know (Lisa, age 43).

For some people, like Lisa, lyrics have little importance in their interpretation of music. More often lyrics were thought of in combination with sounds, or altogether ignored, rather than considered in isolation from other musical elements. The importance of lyrics to audiences, at least in terms of popular music, was diminished in much of the early scholarship in music sociology of the 1950s to 1970s (Frith 1986), and there was continued evidence raised in the 1980s that was used to argue the case that teenagers don't listen to, or don't understand, the lyrics in popular music (e.g. Rosenbaum and Prinsky 1987). Hence, it was contended that the overriding *sound* of the music was the prime reason for its popularity. The balance of musical elements was important to participants presented in this book, for whom the holistic sound of music tended to be communicated almost as much as the lyrics; however, the meaning of this balance is sometimes less clear. Further reference to Frith is important here, when he argues that it is rather the sound, not the lyrical content, that most effectively communicates with listeners:

> It's not just what they sing, but the way they sing it that determines what a singer means to us and how we are placed, as an audience, in relationship to them … it is the sound of the voice, not the words sung, which suggests what a singer really means (1986: 90).

The sound of the voice to which Frith refers here is more accurately described as "timbre", or the character of sound. Timbre can be understood as just one sound, or the result of layers of sound from factors like harmony, rhythm, melody and other aspects like dynamics. DeChaine describes how perceptions of sound may differ with those of lyrics:

> Whereas linguistic signification can undoubtedly provoke emotions and meaning-full experiences, these appear to come by way of reflective cognition. One *thinks* language into meaning and feeling. Sound, by contrast, seems to find a path that traverses or short-circuits conscious reflection … Sound *feels* more deeply, or at least more immediately, than language (2002: 90–91, emphasis original).

What is interesting about this is the often ineffable nature of timbre, even to those familiar with music theory. Like Lisa, many people aren't sure how to describe what they're hearing, perhaps because it is a combination of musical elements, the perception of which is altogether subjective.

Ian, below, was passionate about music for a range of reasons. Here, he spoke about the integration of words and sound in Stevie Wonder's music as the ultimate expression through music:

> 'Living for the City', this, this is one of my favourites here. When this came out I thought, what a song! It's got that same sort of thing where he's not really playing, the notes sort of merge, yeah ... But the words, and the energy, I love it, I love it when they've got this energy and they're really singing – they're desperate. This is meaningful. He means every word of it (Ian, age 60).

Lyrically, Ian explained that he identified with the descriptions of the struggling working class as the subject of the song and that, aesthetically, he felt the music rising up to match the lyrical message. These sympathies within the song and between Ian's life story and the music make it particularly special to him. This kind of connection with music was repeated while listening to Joni Mitchell's 'Coyote':

> I think that guitar there is beautiful, beautiful, but I just love that guitar, it's sort of like, it's you know, it's not strumming a guitar it's just oozing music ... It's beautiful music. That's why I love it, bass, strong bass. And I like the words ... when I taught [high school classes] in 2008 in Mt Isa [Queensland], I was up there without the family or anything – this helped me survive (Ian, age 60).

Ian's evocative language shows the depth of his listening practices, and the love he has for the sounds he hears in this song. Ian drew on a number of elements of this song for emotional support: the lyrics, the drive of the music, and the balance of timbres gave the listener comfort. Attempts to describe the timbre of sound often mean the narrator has to think of new ways of articulating exactly what it is they are hearing. Paul relates his thoughts on timbre to physical sensations:

> My partner actually can't stand Nick Drake, she thinks he's quite dippy in his lyrics and she's right but, yeah ... this particular moment where in a song of his called 'The Thoughts of Mary Jane' which is a pretty dippy kind of stoner song, where it starts just with guitar then a flute comes in and then a full string ensemble comes in, I remember the first time I heard that: "Fuck that's incredible! Musically, that's like someone licking you! Or stroking you all over!" It was quite a physical thing you know, I often get chills, you know like goose bumps in music ... yeah. But uh I don't know how to explain that, that's one of those moments (Paul, age 43).

Some of these sensations are real – the goose bumps or chills – but the others that Paul uses to describe how the music makes him feel are metaphysical and imagined feelings, though to Paul they are an important part of his experience. Remembering and even re-experiencing the feelings first associated with music help to consolidate this music in the lifetime soundtrack. The attraction to timbre in this example is a pleasant surprise for the listener but is one that takes over from the lyrics, which Paul agrees are rather whimsical.

The perception of sound is really the accumulated effect of other musical elements (that are not lyrics or spoken words), traditionally thought of as harmony, melody, rhythm, timbre, texture and dynamics. More often than not, the people I interviewed described sound through reference to timbre, whether this was the collective timbre of the music, or of individual instruments. Vocal tone was one of the most referred to timbres when participants were talking about music in their lifetime soundtrack and deserves some further deliberation. Stella, a vocalist herself, describes her preferences for timbre:

> My favourite stuff to listen to is either soul or gospel kind of stuff or choral music. I think I like black music, pretty much is what I like, black people singing. I like that because, I, it's really emotional. Or I don't even know, it's soulful or something, it has, like, substance to it, I really like listening to the yearning of somebody else in music (Stella, age 22).

Stella's reference to "yearning" suggests that emotion is detectable in the timbres of the human voice, perhaps more so than in instrumental timbres. For many people, the human voice offers a particular level of feeling to music that is not achievable through other mediums. Timbre can act as a strong mnemonic that can persist in memory. Susan recalls her obsession with David Cassidy – an Australian teen heart-throb popular in the 1970s:

> His eyes particularly had me spellbound, he had really pretty eyes, pretty teeth, long hair ... but his song, his voice had ... a gorgeous softness and huskiness to it, that just used to make my heart melt (Susan, age 52).

Cassidy's particular timbre was the aspect that held Susan's attention in the star, evoking the kinds of romanticized affect that are most desired by pop star promoters, and the industry at large. Another participant, Bea, also relayed an ineffable reaction to the human voice:

> I adore Barbara Streisand, I think she's got the most glorious voice, and she can reduce me to tears with ... just the beauty of her voice (Bea, age 81).

As with Susan and Stella, the tone of the voice evokes strong responses that are difficult to describe. These examples illustrate that timbre, as a deeply integrated and essential part of musical sound, plays a key role in the ability for music to capture personal memories through a capacity to express and therefore capture feelings and circumstances for which there are few apt phrases in spoken language.

Rhythm and movement

Our reactions to music may not only be of the mind, but also of the body. Various aspects of music, but particularly rhythm, can incite us to move in response. Head nodding, foot tapping or full coordination of dance, alone or with others, in response to music are all aspects of rhythmic entrainment (Phillips-Silver, Aktipis and Bryant 2010), where rhythms of the body and music synchronize together. Established previously as a key component of musical memories, here the idea of "embodiment" (Van Dijck 2006) becomes literally interpreted through physical reaction and interaction with music. Dance is of course the most obvious and common way in which aspects of music can become embodied. The activity of dancing is particularly special as it involves more than just rhythmic entrainment – coordinated dance engages certain parts of the brain not only for motor skills, but for emotion through the release of endorphins (Laland, Wilkins and Clayton 2016). Dance also has an uncertain evolutionary history and is thought to be a fundamental channel for social communication. It is for these reasons that rhythmic movement can be an integral part of how we experience music that affects the way we create and recall some musical memories.

In Vivian's interview, she ponders on the connection between the types of music recurring in her lifetime soundtrack and her boundless energy for dancing:

> So for me, I really like the beat, and probably because I'm a very structured sort of person ... yeah so probably my taste in music now that I think about it and talk about it aloud is probably because it has the constant predictable beat and I know exactly, so yeah. But I like slow songs too, it's about the beat that gets me wanting to dance (Vivian, age 52).

Many of Vivian's narratives were driven by her recalled feelings and perception of atmosphere, rather than any specific details. Of her reflexive processes, Vivian said she would generally judge "an event on how much I danced or if I enjoyed the music". As such, Vivian's style of forming and reflecting on her musical memories draws strongly on her inclination to embody both music and emotion. Fewer interviewees recalled memories like this, making this participant's fixation on an embodied approach to music engagement fairly unique.

Though dance is the most common idealization of rhythmic movement, it can also manifest in other corporeal patterns that occur concurrently with music. A striking example of this comes in the form of military marching, as described by Vincent, whose thoughts lead him back to his time in the National Service:

> This takes me back to Wacol,[3] on parade, "March!" – "Waltzing Matilda"[4] [sings]. I can never hear that, unless I think I've got a rifle on my shoulder and I'm [makes marching noises], does that make sense? They had other tunes but that's the one that stirred my blood … Well in the military sense, the martial, physical, pounding of your feet and pounding of whatever as you are marching to [sings] "waltzing Matilda, waltzing Matilda!" and you get a high out of that song when you are physically doing something that's you know, stirring you (Vincent, age 77).

There are many sensory aspects to this memory that contribute to the strength of Vincent's association. Particularly, the felt sensations resound in the account – the feeling of a rifle on his shoulder, the position of his arms and shoulders, the pounding of his own and others' timed footfalls. We can imagine the tinny quality of a horn-laden arrangement of 'Waltzing Matilda' blaring from a loudspeaker across the hot, hard surfaces of the parade ground. This music "stirs" Vincent, provoking the repeat of internal feelings – perhaps the churn of the stomach or the resounding of a heartbeat in the ears. This is a powerful memory, linked strongly with the embodiment of music. The repetitious nature of beat and meter somehow help to confer these moments to memory: this music and this movement is engrained in who these people are, stored in the lifetime soundtrack.

Play it back: Technology, consumption and listening

The mediums and listening technologies through which we hear recorded music are obviously the central mechanism allowing music to be duplicated and reproduced. The age range of participants in this research allow for narratives constructed around both old and new technologies, from transistor radios through to magnetic tapes, laser discs, digital files and music streaming, all of which have played a role in shaping lifetime soundtracks. Looking through the memories collected for this research, the significance of playback technologies in the lifetime soundtrack is immense – the radio, cassette or record were often the source and therefore the partial reason for the creation of musical memories in the first instance. The influence of these technologies can be found in nearly all participants' narratives about music and the rapid change of mediums is sometimes reflected on in nostalgic ways, regardless of the quality. Repetition is not only the virtue of technologies for commercial purposes, but also has particular importance in memory processes of formation and reflection. Repeated listening can help embed music over a period of time, as in cloud memories (see Chapter 1). This music can come to characterize a period of time that can stretch for years:

> Yeah it was sort of tied into the adolescence phase ... but I was religiously listening to *Queen Greatest Hits 2* ... cos my sister bought me the tape. We didn't have, despite being really, really, really well off, my parents refused to replace the tape deck in the car with a CD player, so 'oh no first world problems' um but she bought me the greatest hits tape when I was oh must have been 10 I guess ... I still listened to that all the way up til I was you know, 15 so yeah, until I couldn't listen to tapes anymore [laughs]. Oh I loved that tape ... I used to know all the lyrics for every song in the order, and all the keys [laughs] (Matthew, age 26).

Matthew's interaction with music on tape meant that he was in control of playing and replaying music; however, there are many occasions in which the repetition of music is out of the listener's hands. This can happen, for example, in scenarios where music is broadcast to many people at once, such as in shopping centres (think of Christmas carols in your local shopping centre come December), on television, and through patterns of radio airplay. The latter element was central to a memory from Lisa:

> I went through a real phase of Midnight Oil, used to be my absolute favourite band. And [Midnight Oil's] *10 to 1*[5] came out and all that, and I remember Triple J[6] in their test patterns to Brisbane, one of the Midnight Oil Songs was on the test pattern, because they just keep playing the same loop over and over for about a week, and then the station started. I remember that being one of the test songs (Lisa, age 43).

Repetition at the hands of technology is at the heart of this memory – the album to which Lisa refers was released some years previous to its repetition in the test pattern of Triple J radio station. With the assumption that Lisa was already familiar with the album, repeatedly hearing one of these songs herald the arrival of a long-awaited youth station provides a scaffold for the music as part of the lifetime soundtrack.

That participants' narratives often indicate the listening medium suggests the importance of the technology of original listening experiences. This includes the physicality of interacting with that technology – setting up record players, and handling CDs without scratching are skills that form part of our habitual remembering habits as they are enacted through the body in everyday life (Anderson 2004). These habits have an affective component too, as van Dijck elaborates:

> Incontrovertibly, the materiality of recorded music influences the process of remembering ... Music listened to from live radio, records, cassette tapes, or mp3 players has a different emotion attached to it ... Hearing a familiar song on the radio constitutes a different memory experience than playing that very song from one's own collection (2006: 366).

For many participants in this research, the original medium through which they listened to music in the lifetime soundtrack forms an integral part of the recalled sound. This has subsequent effects on how it is recalled in memory but can also create a gap when music is played in newer formats with higher fidelity. Such formats can provide a closer examination of original sounds and deliver a different experience to new listeners, because, as Bennett (2008: 265) offers,

> [The] CD both "freezes" sound [of the late 1960s and 1970s] in its pristine state whilst at the same time bringing out the particular contingencies and peculiarities of sound recording that helped to frame certain rock albums as historical documents, situated in particular contexts of time, place, technology, and creative licence.

While there are some benefits in the fidelity of re-released or remastered recordings, it is possible that such sounds may not generate the same affect as before. With the rise in vinyl consumer culture since the early 2000s, recreating original affect – at least of records – is achievable for some. The aesthetic quality of vinyl interacts with both old and new markets of consumers: the older generation, for elements of nostalgic experience, and for youth markets in which vinyl holds particular cultural capital (see Bartmanski and Woodward 2015). Taking advantage of what has now become very affordable technology ranging in quality, Paul set about finding a particular "authentic" listening aesthetic:

> I recently found a record player, 20 bucks, it's pretty bad, but one of the first records ... one of the most important records that was important for me to get was *Bridge Over Troubled Water* [by Simon and Garfunkel] because even as I recall that album, I recall the tape that I made of that album that I taped off ... the LP which had scratches and clicks and stuff, it had skips at certain moments in the songs so even now when I listen to those songs I'm expecting those clicks to still be there (Paul, age 43).

Paul's memories of this album are based on a tape recording that includes the audio artefacts of either his, or someone else's, vinyl record. The result is that the sounds of the recorded music are mediated through the tape – though this would suffer a lack of fidelity associated with cassettes. This experience has informed his expectations of what the record is meant to sound like, according to his memory. Even though he is hearing, in the present, a new record, it lacks the same pattern of crackles that he could discern on the tape: so powerful are these subtleties.

Music in the late twentieth century and beyond, as Kassabian (2013) has established, is everywhere: accessible at any time, in many locations. Recorded music can be accessed immediately, and often virtually for free through both legal and illegal downloading. In comparison to their younger counterparts, older generations had limited access to recorded music and it could be supposed that as a result, they have fewer memorialized listening experiences than younger people. On the contrary, rather than limiting the effectiveness of the lifetime soundtrack, a restricted engagement as described by older participants may place a greater emphasis on the access to music within their memories. Their descriptions of waiting to hear music display a sense of patience when compared to the modern pervasion of music into every sphere of life. Perhaps the increasing availability of music and instantaneous access on a range of devices even has the effect of diluting the meaning of music and its significance in autobiographical experiences.

Certainly, this saturation of music in daily life can, and will, alter lifetime soundtracks into the future. The effects of this were revealed in interviews with younger people, who often described a listening habit consisting of song mixes or compilations – either created by them, or for them using streaming platform algorithms. This turn away from album-led listening could result in less cloud memories relating to whole albums, and *ipso facto*, shorter periods of time being associated with single songs. The ability for digital music players or streaming services to skip or randomly order songs from one or a range of artists may encourage a more chaotic and indiscriminate listening style and is leading to what Bennett and Rogers describe as an "immateriality" in music (2016), where the physical artefacts of musical memory are becoming less common. These changes are interesting, but they do not preclude the formulation of the lifetime soundtrack through everyday listening. Music released in modern formats still has the capacity to trigger memory through the static replication of musical elements, if not to a greater degree than previously. At the same time, we should not bemoan the advances of music technology, for it is due to this that the lifetime soundtrack can be both created and consolidated.

The musical memory vault

As a final thought on the ways in which music helps to catalogue memory as per an archive, there are some arguments in memory studies and psychology that music can reach those memories that have very nearly been forgotten or are recalled rarely. Psychological descriptions of these kinds of memories sometimes refer to their state as "repressed": the blocking of certain events from memory can occur in response to severe trauma (Loftus 1993). Recall of these memories can be prompted by external triggers, the basis of which can be found in the original event (Elliott 1997: 812). Though the people engaged for this research did not express a connection with music and severely traumatic or painful memories, there were suggestions that music could act as a trigger for memories that were deeply buried in their psyche, perhaps as a result of high emotional content, or the singular nature of the event.

Vincent describes below an instance of music triggering a decidedly sensitive moment:

> There is a piece of music which is done at military funerals. Don't hear it very often, but drums and whatever … you hear it occasionally at a royal funeral or something. When I hear that I'm taken back to the funeral of a very good friend of mine who was killed in an accident in the army … national service, when we were doing a follow-up for training. When I hear that, I'm at that funeral, feeling very, very, very sad, very, very upset … It's not the sort of thing I find easily recalled, it takes the music to make me recall it (Vincent, age 77).

Vincent's memory for this event is triggered only upon hearing the music, bringing with it a torrent of emotion. To this end, there is a degree to which such memories may be purposefully suppressed by individuals, rather than being unconsciously repressed, to avoid reliving unwelcome thoughts, visions and feelings. Reasons for this memory lying dormant for long periods of time might also lie in the music itself: Vincent mentions that the music he experienced at this event was typically reserved for certain occasions. The nature of the music used for events such as military funerals engages with a traditional custom and stimulates a sense of collective reverence. With the music seldom being replayed in Vincent's day-to-day life, and ostensibly, all other reminders of this time also rarely re-appearing, the memory itself remains stored but relatively dormant in the mind. This is not an isolated case – other participants also told of avoiding certain music where possible, to stem the tide of memories that may come with it (see Chapter 3).

Although the affective nature of Vincent's story is rather sombre in tone, dormant memories do not always comprise something akin to suppressed traumas and can instead be benign thoughts that are rather a curiosity of the mind. One such memory surfaced when conversing with Jeremy, whose recollection of purchasing a Guns N' Roses album unfolded as he continued talking:

> [I remember] just the sort of waiting and anticipation of any new music they ever put out which is long and far between with them. It was painful, but I remember they were gonna release the *Use Your*

> *Illusion* albums one and two at the same time, and um, it was liter-
> ally years between them because I was in high school by the time they
> actually released them and when they finally had the release date for
> them, me and my friend … we went down, pre-ordered it, and the
> day it came out we were waiting for "CD Mickey's" to open and we
> went and got our CDs, came back to my place and we listened to
> them back to back – sat on my couch and listened to them back to
> back the whole thing. We were both massive, massive Guns N' Roses
> fans, still are, both of us. Yeah, now I remember sitting on the couch
> and sort of thinking about it and how much I liked it, what I liked
> about it, what I didn't like about it, stuff like that (Jeremy, age 36).

Jeremy's memory is drawn out from the initial feelings associated with these albums – a sense of anticipation, which led to the actions of pre-ordering copies so there was no chance he could miss out on hearing this music on the same day as other fans. This leads on to a sense-laden memory of sitting on a familiar couch, surrendering to a dedicated listening session, and the discussion that followed. This memory is important, because Guns N' Roses have played an influential part in Jeremy's lifetime soundtrack, though the distinct activities that led to actually hearing the music for the first time were tucked away, perhaps overshadowed by later experiences with these albums or songs within.

The idea that music keeps strong, if not frequently used, bonds with memory has also been discussed in the use of music-based therapies with dementia-affected individuals. Reports, both anecdotal and scholarly, suggest patients which other stimulus, in that music can stimulate or enhance the recollection of memories in dementia cluding the faces of family members, cannot (Belfi, Karlan and Tranel 2016; El Haj *et al.* 2015). It has been argued that the pathway between memory and music is one of the last connections to be affected by the disease, while there is some emerging evidence that the connection may even be spared altogether (Cuddy and Duffin 2005). There is much ongoing research that seeks to establish the link between memory and music in this cognitive capacity, and as yet there are few studies to show any link between certain musical elements and memory recall in dementia. Nonetheless, the persistence of memories associated with music despite the damages of dementia and associated memory diseases is indicative of the strength with which the connections between these two agents are made.

Live music: Autobiographical experience and the collective

While a good deal of this chapter has been devoted to the role of recorded music in personal archiving to the exclusion of live music, this is not to say that live music does not interact with memory. Undoubtedly, seeing an idol playing one's favourite songs in real time can become an extremely memorable music experience (see Gabrielsson 2011). Furthermore, seeing music performed live is often more emotional than listening to recorded music, due to the visual stimulation of performance, the venue, and the presence of others (Coutinho and Scherer 2017). Live music experiences are rarely able to be relived through the music itself (with the exception of personal recordings made at the event) and persist only in memory. While this might prevent live music from producing a personal memory index in exactly the same way as recorded music, it does play a role in situating individual experience within the collective, and in so doing, influences our perception of the lifetime soundtrack.

The performance of music to an audience for their enjoyment, contrasting with conditions of rehearsal or examination, usually occurs before a group of people: it is rare that an audience would consist of only one person, such is the social function of music. Indeed, attending a concert with hundreds or thousands of others has been a regular practice for centuries, exacerbated at times by the repurposing of large venues, like sports stadiums, for the execution of a live event hosting tens of thousands of audience members. What is particularly interesting in this context is the overlap of individual and collective worlds: the music is being transferred to large numbers of people, who are all present in similar ways; however, each person is interpreting the music according to their own sense of experience and identity. In this way, the live concert is something of a literal representation of listening to recorded music in the globalized era of music production. While you are listening to the music through headphones and comprehending it in relation to your own experiences (with music or otherwise), so too are potentially thousands, or millions, of other people around the world.

So, is the experience of the live music concert individual or collective in nature? And how does it function within the lifetime soundtrack? Narrated sharing of live music experience can become a method for connecting with music communities across time and space through the recognition of shared experience and individual reception. In the digital age, this kind of sharing is increased through the advent of online forums and archives in which people can relate their retrospective thoughts on music, artists, specific concerts and venues, increasing the collective nature of music experience. Nonetheless, we each can take something personal and intimate away from shared events, which must negotiate a special relationship with other musical memories within the lifetime soundtrack.

Conclusion

This chapter has explored several new theories regarding the relationship between music and memory. Specifically, these theories can be reasonably applied to recorded music, but are more complex when looking at music experienced in live contexts. Looking closely into participants' memory narratives and opinions on music allows an application of the idea that music, and moreover, elements of music and music experience can be thought of as "memory places" which capture experiences and index them in the lifetime soundtrack. Lyrics are particularly effective in articulating thoughts, feelings and even specific situations that may be difficult for the listener to otherwise explain or may in fact help the listener realize and express themselves. Textures and timbres work alongside any vocal aspect of music, or otherwise are at the forefront of the subjective qualities of sound a listener may perceive. Timbre is especially enigmatic – often itself difficult to describe, the very sound of an instrument, and often a voice, can help to encapsulate the atmosphere, sentiments or circumstances of an event in our memory. There was little mention of other musical elements from participants: melody and harmony remain outstanding in the particular roles they might play in capturing the mnemonic imagination.

In considering extra-musical elements, this chapter described the effects of rhythm and movement, where dance or other forms of musical embodiment can act as scaffolding measures in aiding the storage of musical memories. This is an aspect of memorialization – the process of remembering – that incorporates both the body and the mind in specialized ways. Playback technology was highlighted as central to the music-memory relationship, where it allows the creation and recreation of memories through the provision of recorded and replicable music. Significantly, mediums and technologies of music can affect the way music is remembered in the lifetime soundtrack – the crackles, pops, rough edges and nuances of certain listening modes may endure in memory, refusing to be replaced by versions of higher fidelity. The replication of musical elements presented by recorded music offers the second crux of the proposed theories between music and memory: that music can help to reproduce memories more faithfully, given the natural tendencies of remembering and forgetting to fluctuate over time.

These ideas are a step forward in understanding more broadly the ways we connect with music through memory, and vice versa. However, this is only one form of remembering, and music is only one of many cultural forms that regularly interact with memory. This one, then, serves as a beginning in what could be a broad, interdisciplinary argument about the functions and integration of culture and autobiographical memory. Further, something that was not mentioned in this chapter, because it often was not discussed in participant interviews, was the pathways taken up between memory and music that people *don't like*. In the above excerpts, people are mostly speaking about aspects of their favourite music, or reasons why they feel empathy or attachment to music. It is important to remember that the lifetime soundtrack is not only made up of music we like or regularly listen to out of choice: a good deal of the soundtrack consists of music that we come across that makes a mark in our memory somehow; whether we perceive that as positive or negative has only a small influence over whether it will appear in our soundtrack. It is plausible that similar relationships are at play when forming musical memories either with music we don't like, or music we have come to dislike by association, though there is more work at hand to define this with further clarity. In sum, this chapter has offered a conceptualization of music, not as an archive for memory, but as an index in which are elements of music and music experience. Though it is not a flawless system, this index helps to create what, over time, becomes the lifetime soundtrack, validated by the continuing exchange between music and memory in everyday life.

Notes

1.   For example, when The Beatles' recordings were remastered in 2009, the true key of songs was revealed where original recording tapes were adjusted to align with standard A440 pitch.

2.   Refers to 'What a Wonderful World' written by George David Weiss and George Douglas, made famous by Louis Armstrong ('Satchmo') in 1967.

3.   Wacol is a suburb of Brisbane, Queensland, which hosted 'Camp Columbia', a facility for American and Australian troops in military camps during World War Two.

4.   A traditional Australian folk song.

5.   Refers to album *10, 9, 8, 7, 6, 5, 4, 3, 2, 1* released by Midnight Oil in 1982. Triple J was one of the first radio stations to play Midnight Oil's music, before they went on to have high levels of commercial success.

6.   National youth radio station Triple J began broadcasting in Brisbane in 1989.

5 Effects of Music-Making on Musical Memories and the Lifetime Soundtrack

The implication embedded in the term "lifetime soundtrack" is that it comprises music one has come across through listening, by sharing music with others or retreating into personal soundscapes in the bedroom or through headphones. For many though, listening is only one way in which they engage with music, for the activity of making music is as prevalent as ever, with the rise of DIY musicianship and increasing online resources for self-tuition. As such, music-making, and the products thereof, can inform the lifetime soundtrack in significant ways. Musicianship itself can occur on a scale from amateur through to professional levels of practice, through which deepening knowledge of music gives way to a greater awareness of the tools of music's composition, the technology of recording, and the effects of performing on the self and others. Playing an instrument or singing also invokes processes that have benefits for both the body and brain; besides this, the specialized use of the body and brain makes for an engagement with music that contrasts with listening alone. Hence, there is more to remember: there are different sensations, mind-sets, and other contexts that mean memories for making music infuse the content of the lifetime soundtrack with a unique range of encounters.

The typical activities of music – composing, rehearsing, performing – require people who participate in music-making to engage with music in diverse ways (Becker 1951). The narratives of interviewees who participated in music-making offer some insights into how this affects the lifetime soundtrack, especially where they bear foundational differences to narratives from those whose main musical pursuit was listening. Beyond a discussion of amateur and professional musicians, the focus in this chapter turns to the effect of musicianship on listening where musical and para-musical knowledge might affect the comprehension or appreciation of music. Attention then shifts to the connections between personal identity and musicianship. In particular, the perception of music-making as "work" as opposed to leisure, especially for professional musicians, and the effect of this on identity is brought to the fore. Music can constitute a "working identity" in situations where either the performer is being paid for their services, or when an individual's attitude to the performance reflects feelings of displeasure or boredom. If performers or composers view music-making as a key part of their identity, especially if it is their vocation, this may affect the lens through which they remember and reflect upon their lifetime soundtrack.

The chapter also considers the performance of emotion, which sees musicians affecting those around them while also needing to manage how they might feel personally. This can influence the way music is remembered and means musicians must shift their approach between the objectification of music where it is seen as work, and the significance of personally meaningful performance. In order to carry out performances that create desired affects for audiences, musicians need to work on their manipulation of sounds through the body, drawing on a knowledge of typical responses and notions of authenticity. This too may alter how music may become associated with memory, via the designation of emotion that is suggested or personally perceived. Finally, the integration of physical and spiritual manifestations of music embodiment is explored for the deeper effects of music on its performers. The physicality of the body that both instrumentalists and vocalists enact when they produce music is an outward manifestation of musical embodiment (Maslen 2013). Such action not only aids emotional expression within performance, it also plays on a deep-seated engagement with music. Alongside the mastery of technical practice can also come a more innate sense of musicality, one that is more intensely connected with a player's maturing understanding of music and their performance thereof. When performing, musicians can intimately experience the creation of music in a way that is relatively inaccessible for others. This is perhaps the most exclusive aspect of musicianship to influence the creation of musical memories, where the knowledge of personal music production can be incorporated into memories that also include other contexts and emotions. If these principles affect the way musicians encounter and comprehend music in everyday situations, then they also have the potential to affect the way music is integrated with autobiographical memories and the lifetime soundtrack.

Music participation: Amateurs and professionals

The level of investment one can have in their craft has been characterized through a range of terminology, including dabblers, hobbyists or amateurs, and those in the pursuit of "serious leisure" (Gates 1991; Stebbins 1992). Despite this, there seems to be a reticence to take a firm stance on what characteristics lead to the use of the descriptor of "musician". Jorgensen (1993: 43) states that the variance in terms used for musicians should align with the individual's view of music as one of (i) work (professional/amateur), (ii) serious leisure (amateurs/hobbyists) or (iii) play (recreationists or dabblers). A subject of less debate is the idea raised by Jorgensen that a professional musician is one who earns a living from music, with which most scholars and practitioners agree. Yet the characterization of a musician who may perform occasionally and has received vernacular (as opposed to institutionalized) training remains up for discussion. The amateur or hobbyist may still take their engagement with music very seriously, despite it not making up any or a substantial part of their income (Juniu, Tedrick and Boyd 1996: 46) – many entertainers may hold an unrelated day job to deal with the high cost of modern living. Drummond (1990) and Juniu and colleagues (1996) agree that an individual can embody concepts of both professional and amateur, depending on their motivations. Participants in my research self-identified as amateurs or professionals, or something in between, playing original compositions, jazz standards, or popular music covers. Many had a high level of musical training through institutions, but others progressed their practice outside of other work. Not represented here are people who occupy more modern or peripheral roles, such as DJs and audio engineers, though it is equally likely that people in these roles would have a unique relationship with music that could align with the guiding concepts of this chapter, perhaps with an even greater emphasis on listening technologies.

The experience of one participant, Ron, highlights that the categorization of amateur musician is not always fair. Sometimes this tag suggests that the pursuit of musical skill is limited at the discretion of the person in question, when in reality, restrictions in musical training can be imposed by external forces, like needing to provide for a family through a profession with a salary. On being a musician, Ron says:

> It's like carrying a big boulder around on your shoulders. It's not all been good, it's not good because it's something you want to become better at, it's something you want to hear more of … and it's more of a burden sometimes. That's to me personally, I don't know if everybody feels that way. Because you're not perfect and you haven't perfected it, and you were instructed the wrong way. As a child, I was given bad direction (Ron, age 59).

As other memory narratives will demonstrate, the practice of music has complex effects on the sense of self. Ron describes the pressure of not feeling good enough at his instrument, and later tells of frustration at not having the capacity to practice more often. Certainly, to be provided music training and to take up continued study is dependent on external factors such as encouragement, opportunity (which sometimes also indicates privilege), attitude and skills (Pitts 2016). In particular, older generations in Australia may not have had the access to equipment and tuition, and even current generations can be prohibited from extensive musical training due to remote geographical location. Besides this, music training is not guaranteed to be a positive experience nor one that generates welcome memories (Hallam 2010; Smith 2008). For example, participant Ryan found that he was encouraged to listen to complex music for the benefit of his saxophone practice at a young age:

> I think there is music that I avoid ... sort of early on when I was learning sax I got into the whole John Coltrane thing, John Coltrane, Charlie Parker – 'cause you know you pretty much have to listen to that stuff – but I think at that age I wasn't really ready to sort of listen to it. I didn't really understand enough about it, so I'd listen to it 'cause I had to, and um and sort of I didn't enjoy it as much and then even to this day I *could* enjoy listening to Coltrane, but I just don't tend to as much just because ... of those associations (Ryan, age 20).

This adverse association with music can be recalled by the act of listening, but also by Ryan's continued interaction with his instrument. The music of John Coltrane – which for Ryan and many other jazz students is closely bound to the discourse of jazz saxophone – is harder to avoid in Ryan's practice as a musician, than if the music were unrelated to his everyday activities.

Training in music has been shown to enhance a wide range of cognitive functions, including the perception of speech and development of language skills and literacy, along with numeracy, intellectual development and physical and mental well-being (Hallam 2010), which may further contribute to the integration of music and memory. Participating with others, especially within ensembles like choirs, can have a range of positive effects on social, emotional and mental well-being (Clift and Hancox 2010; Stewart and Lonsdale 2016) and may also have a place in memory. An initial experience of making music with others has stuck with Vincent for over 60 years:

> I survived Nudgee Junior and then in 1949 I went, became a scholarship student at Nudgee Senior at Nudgee College Boondall.[1] Life was different there, they were more civilized. They did have a magnificent chapel and they did have a practice of singing every Sunday, very – shall we say – broad range of hymns, 'Faith of Our Fathers', 'Soul of my Saviour'. I can never hear any of those without being back in that chapel, because that's the first time I ever had any participatory music where you're doing it with a lot of folk you know. Later on, they formed the formal choir, which they had to lead in high mass, which was celebrated about three times a year. And that's when we sung Joseph Smith's Mass in C, which had part singing in, all sorts of things, I don't hear it at all any more but if ever I do hear [*sings in Latin*] immediately – I'm back in that chapel (Vincent, age 77).

Though the first experience is striking for Vincent, singing with others became a highly enjoyable activity such that the collective experiences over his time at the college can be condensed into a vivid set of sights, sounds and smells that embody music-making in the chapel setting.

As far as the lifetime soundtrack is concerned, I haven't set out to argue that musicians have a higher quality or more extensive soundtrack: in the experience of hobbyists, professionals, and those with little musical training, the lifetime soundtrack remains a record of music that they have encountered that holds an enduring association with a singular memory or set of memories. And in fact, there are also many ways in which people who do and don't participate in music-making are quite similar. For example, there is evidence that both parties are equally affected by the aesthetics of music (Madsen *et al.* 1993). As the bulk of music sociology scholarship describes, many people, be they musicians or not, have strong ties with music and see it as part of their personal identity and as a way of fitting into, or standing out from, a collective (Frith 1987). Rather, the variance explored here is one found in the creation of musical memories, where musicians are either applying specialized knowledge, or performing the music in question.

Musicians as music consumers

> Live music experience is somewhat different, but I think I probably listen to more recorded music than I ever have live music, and I've probably played more live music than I've ever experienced as an audience member (Paul, age 42).

Every person who lent their memory narratives to this research could be described as a consumer of music – and, perhaps, almost everyone reading this book is highly likely to fit this role as well. Simply listening can be thought of as consuming in a traditional sense, and in a business sense, one who buys music (in recorded form, or via concert tickets) constitutes the end user – the consumer, the person for whom the music was likely produced. Those who understand themselves to be musicians in one way or another can take on the role of music consumer, insofar as listening is considered a part of consumption, as well as the role of "music performer", as per Paul, above. An intimate knowledge of their own instrument as well as others provides them with an understanding of what it takes to create certain sounds and atmospheres in both live situations and the recording studio. First-hand experience with music technology as a recording musician may bring an element of personalized analysis to their listening. This was something discussed by Tony:

> I remember the first time I heard Blood, Sweat & Tears that was
> you know another life changer, because [it was] very, very sophis-
> ticated, it was recorded in a completely new way. Very clean, close
> to the mic drum sound that they hadn't [used] before, so that was
> a serious big moment (Tony, age 62).

This memory seems to be significant for Tony in two ways; the leading aspect
is that this is described as a "first experience", which suggests it is remembered
because it was a critical point in his encounters with music over his lifetime.
In combination with this, Tony was attuned not only to the sounds he was
hearing, but how they were created within the recording process, which was
for him a particularly interesting factor. These aspects together make this listening experience an enduring musical memory, one that, given the approxi-
mate time period of this experience, has remained a peak encounter through
many similar occurrences over time.

In an example that resonates with Tony's story, James's knowledge of production styles provided him with opportunities for analytical listening experiences. Now a part-time sessional musician, as a young adult James was
involved in several bands that performed regularly around Brisbane in the
1990s. Gaining popularity around this time was the musical genre of grunge;
below, James recounts his original encounter with Nirvana:

> The first time I heard Nirvana was at Dooley's Hotel[2] when it was
> a live venue, and it came on and we all just sort of went, "Wow
> what's that sound?" It was a really, really interesting sound. Um,
> and at the end, it was the first one off *Nevermind*, 'Teen Spirit', just
> the sound of it was something, it was so impressive, such a wall of
> sound … I remember just being there and the guys in my band we
> were just floored by the sound, and that whole wall of sound thing
> came, they're not the first ones to do it, but the first ones to really
> – when they knocked Michael Jackson off the charts in the States
> you just go "wow" that's just huge, a couple of grunge heads you
> know. So that was pretty impressive (James, age 41).

Like Tony, the recognition of new aesthetic sounds comes as a welcome surprise that acts as a critical point of recall in later life. The narrative exemplifies the reaction of a group of knowledgeable musicians who are in the first
instance drawn to the production value of the sound, rather than any other
aspect of the music.

An album presented to someone learning an instrument can be scrutinized
for all it has to offer an apt pupil. These songs become tied into memory not
only because of the repetition of the music but for the distinct tones and timbres
focused on by the listener. Sometimes, as described by Matthew below, listening experiences can become instructive and may influence a musician's practice.

> There's a CD [that my Mum] just randomly went out and saw this ballads album and just handed me this album of tenor sax ballads. And there was a track on that, which I still listen to, Ben Webster playing 'Stardust' and it's a really particular ... version ... I really got into Ben Webster, so his version of that and ah a Duke Ellington tune called 'Single Petal of a Rose'. Ben Webster is known for his very airy sort of tone and [I] really got into his sort of tone, and he's a great tenor player and I was an alto player, so I was trying to emulate this ridiculous tone on an alto, which is just super bright and thin, and couldn't do it but I spent ages trying to do that (Matthew, age 25).

While ultimately Matthew's pursuit of Webster's tone was somewhat fruitless given the difference in instruments, the memory continues to connect his experiences of both listening to and playing music. Matthew reflected fondly on the album as a whole, with several tracks continuing to tie in with his musical development on saxophone. This kind of memory is important in the sense that autobiographical reflection on the smaller details that shape our lives can help to consolidate a sense of self, and to confirm or refute the decisions made in the past.

Identity: Working as a performer

Though the characterization of professional and amateur musicians is problematized in the literature, it is important to recognize that personal perceptions of musical involvement can also influence musical memory. One aspect that may alter this is the way someone thinks about the role music plays in their life. If producing, composing or performing music was considered *work* rather than leisure, and if one encountered music in sometimes problematic circumstances, such a discourse would frame life experience with music in particular ways. When music is thought of as work, the same issues that disrupt other careers can also cause a disjuncture between music performance as pleasurable, and music performance as repetitive, fatigue-inducing, or uninspiring.

Despite the fact that scholars such as Jorgensen (1993), and Junui and colleagues (1996) argue amateur musicians perceive rehearsal and performance as leisure while professional musicians are more likely to think of this as work, the interchange between paid and unpaid activities of this nature make the concept of music as "work" more complex (Finnegan 2007). For example, a musician may do unpaid rehearsals for a paid gig or may occasionally perform for less than what is considered standard compensation, or even for free. The significance in people choosing music as a career lies in the effects this can have on personal identity. As described through studies by social anthropologists and sociologists such as Finnegan (2007), Becker (1951;

Faulkner and Becker 2009), and Cohen (1991), music for musicians is part of the "working self" – it is the activity by which performers may earn (some part of) their wage, as well as contributing to a social identity that differs to that of a consumer. Hence, when personal identity is closely tied to music-making and music performance, music in the lifetime soundtrack may relate to autobiographical memory in deeply composite ways. For Tony, music has featured throughout his life:

> Being a lifelong professional musician, born of professional musician parents, it's obviously been at the forefront of my life and still working in music but not as a performer, it's a constant presence, and probably more important than anything non-personal. For me relationships are the most important thing, but probably after relationships music would have had the biggest impact on my life (Tony, age 62).

The creative ideals of music-making make music as work, in comparison to some other vocations, seem to comprise a glamorous and enviable job. At the same time, the performance of music, especially when this is carried out nightly or weekly, can present the same troubles as any other kind of regular work: fatigue and boredom can result from repetitive tasks. When performing for others in the circumstances of work, a musician takes on a service role, which may require the display or management of "appropriate emotions" also known as "emotional labour" (Ashforth and Humphrey 1993; Hochschild 2003), the potential consequence of which Hochschild (2003) identifies as alienation from the action or activity utilized in the work itself.

Examining emotional labour across the creative industries, Hesmondhalgh and Baker (2010, 2011) describe a tension between creativity, engaged or disengaged audiences and the dollar amount for each gig. For example, interviewees in their research spoke of the reduced need to play in particularly innovative or novel ways if their music serves only an atmospheric need: there is a demand here to appear outwardly engaged with the performance despite the performer feeling undervalued or emotionally disconnected. Even if the circumstances in which a musician is performing are joyful for others, such feelings may not be quite the same for the player. As Ryan flippantly quips:

> Like it was just a gig, it was pretty detached, you know – had this music, played it, got my 300 bucks (Ryan, age 20).

Such feelings of disconnect may relate to the style of music played: participants in McMillan's (2015) research into performer identity expressed a lower level of gratification when performing cover music, over original compositions. One of my participants, James, an instrumental technician and full-time musician, explained how he stopped playing rock and pop cover music during his career due to decreased enjoyment:

> I did years and years of covers music and stuff like that and I just don't find it exciting anymore, at all. I don't really want to do that again (James, age 41).

In scenes where cover music is in greater demand than original music, or where musicians can make more money from playing such gigs, repetition (playing at the same venues, and/or playing similar tunes on a regular basis) becomes the defining factor in intensifying emotional labour. James began splitting his wage between working as a tradesman to provide steady support for his family, while continuing to perform with select original music groups. Ostensibly, the practice of music-making must also offer individuals some personal sense of fulfilment. The typical financial hardships with which music-based careers are stigmatized infer some form of deep attraction between a musician and their craft, bringing to mind characterizations of the "starving artist". Music can therefore serve multiple yet conflicting purposes. As Matthew puts it:

> [Music is] an outlet for emotions I guess … probably the simplest way to put it. I guess now it's even more important than ever 'cause it's how I make money [laughs]. So not only is it an emotional outlet – back then it was just purely for that – now it's also financial (Matthew, age 25).

The need to make money from something that is also a source of pleasure introduces a suite of issues that can complicate musicians' attitudes towards music. Looking to jazz musicians, Becker (1951) describes a particular frustration of the need to earn money, which was most often achieved by playing on gigs for corporate events, where the requested repertoire is considered too mainstream or kitsch. This involved "playing for squares": people who neither understand nor appreciate the artistry involved in music-making, especially jazz, which further scaffolds the idea of musical activity as *work*.

A pertinent example of this was unintentionally provided again by Matthew, who described his emotional engagement with his work in the corporate music scene:

> I guess I'm de-sensitized to a lot of weddings 'cause I've played at a lot of them and you hear the same songs … "Oh I can't believe you asked me to play 'Girl from Ipanema' for your wedding waltz – that doesn't make sense. It's in four and you want me to play it as a swing and it's a Latin tune, and it's about a girl who's too stuck up to look at a dude." So, you know, I'm pretty de-sensitized to the whole wedding sort of thing (Matthew, age 25).

The tune Matthew refers to, made famous by Astrud Gilberto and Antonio Carlos Jobim in the Latin jazz wave of the 1960s is, in the eyes of many modern jazz performers, an over-played and underwhelming standard they loathe to perform. The narrative here describes a perceived musical ignorance as a source of frustration: hence musical knowledge is also altering the way the participant is thinking about, and remembering, the music. Here too, elements of creativity are seized by the employer, reflecting again Becker's observations. Matthew's description of the song suggests that it occupies a plurality of forms in his lifetime soundtrack, and has strong associations with memories of work, rather than leisure.

These narratives lend some credence to the notion that seeing interaction with music as "work" can affect the way music is perceived and memorialized. Though payment for performance seems to be at the heart of these musicians' issues, further problems could arise for work that is not paid, but expected, such as in community groups or families. There is a common theme evident here, where performers detach emotionally in order to perform in service to others, which is worth noting for its influence on musical memories in the lifetime soundtrack. The following section seeks more clarity on the prevalence of emotional labour in performance, as well as the impact of musical affect on the performer.

Performance and management of emotion

In her work on emotional labour, Hochschild (2003: 7) observes that emotion is often *managed* in service roles to create "a publicly observable facial and bodily display". As already alluded to above, this can occur in music-making especially where an apparent engagement with music is put on in order to appease employers and to gain paid employment. The role of emotion in music-making runs somewhat deeper than just this interface between private and public lives. Emotion is present in various ways, from an understanding of emotive performance elements, to the rewards of practice and engagement with others (Woody 2002; Woody and McPherson 2010). Aspects of music as work aside, a performer can both produce affect for others, but need to make decisions about the execution of the emotion, such that they are not overly affected by it themselves.

In performing music designed to signify or allow listeners to feel or express emotion, a performer may need to disconnect from emotional elements for the benefit of the performance. As Stella describes:

> Unfortunately, I sing at funerals quite regularly, so I would have sung at like sixty, I don't know, sixty-plus. And I do it kind of regularly like one a fortnight maybe ... poor choice of words for funerals but it's like, dead to me ... I don't feel emotional ... That's probably

> just because I try and turn off so much, because I do not want to get
> involved. They pay me to do it, so I do not want to blubber down
> in mucus in the middle of a funeral (Stella, age 22).

Stella's experience demonstrates the combination of emotion, music and memory from the perspective of performer and listener. While those hearing the music may later form strong emotional associations to the music based on the circumstance, it is likely that the musician might remember the event in a different way. Two types of emotion processing are recognized in music psychology: "induced" emotion describes an emotional response in reaction to music, whereas "perceived" emotion denotes the recognition of affect in music without actually experiencing that feeling (van Zijl and Sloboda 2010). The latter is used to great effect by Stella, who can still provide an ostensibly sensitive performance, without becoming affected herself. Perhaps this kind of dissociation is enacted to safeguard the practice of music from the intrusion of other aspects of life and vice versa.

Self-identified hobbyist, Ron, has developed a protective approach to music-making:

> Mmm, yeah I've got a day job, I've gotta work, so I can't get emo-
> tionally involved in something, that I can't do because I can't do it
> properly – professionally – because I'm not good enough to do it
> professionally. So what I've gotta do well is earn money and live.
> What I then do for a hobby is play music the best I can, practice,
> and listen to music. So I've got two lives (Ron, age 59).

What Ron is describing is a conflict between the pleasure of music-making and what he sees as an indulgence of emotional investment in a practice that does not earn a wage. Ron is effectively managing his emotions to combat the perpetual tug of leisure versus labour, where his daily job is entirely separate from his musical pursuits. Such is the choice of many musicians who bear the label of amateur or hobbyist, where it is not financially viable to take up music as a profession. Nonetheless, felt emotion in response to music is not always avoidable. Tony aptly describes the inevitable effects of music:

> So I'm totally conscious … of what techniques that you can apply
> to try and ah, get people to respond in particular ways, but it still
> works, you know. I s'pose it's like knowing a Nurofen[3] is going to
> stop a headache – it doesn't stop it from working. But for me, you
> know, [being a musician] doesn't protect you from being affected
> by it (Tony, age 62).

In fact, many musicians I spoke with did have emotional experiences in their own performances, with the main difference with the above narratives being that the performance was for, or became associated with, events or people significant to the performer, and with music that resonated with personal preferences. Stella, above, describes her experiences performing at funerals for her local church. In other narratives, performance at funerals came up again, but in the following instances, the deceased was a close family member.

> [Mum] just passed away, last year. So, that was a very strong connection ... I always tell the story how she you know, she was a great one for practising unconditional love and the only condition she placed on me was to sing 'What a Wonderful World'[4] at her service. And I said "Oh yeah Mum, I'll do that, but what happens if I go first?" And so I had a pact that she was to sing at my funeral – anyway, I got to sing at hers and so 'Wonderful World' is a very important song, in a number of ways, because she placed that condition on me, I threw it back at her, but then I got to – did get to – sing it at her service. So yeah ... 'cause she was um, she was beautiful (George, age 66).

While the song might be significant to George and his mother in recorded form, his performance of it adds an extra dimension to his mnemonic associations: this is something that is particular to the way musicians can embellish their musical memories. The song is also a signifier of the relationship between mother and son, where its part in their mutual pact gives the song overt, inscribed meaning.

Felt emotion as a result of music-making can also manifest as a result of problems emerging within or around performance. James toured with high-level rock acts in his role as drum technician, but at one point in his career the involvement with this life became too much:

> I actually really hated music for a while ... yeah Powderfinger did the Big Day Out tour one year ... Slipknot were on the stage and System of a Down then Powderfinger ... the noise was so loud ... they played for an hour and then System of a Down were on almost instantly for an hour, and then Powderfinger and it was just like, it was just brain numbing. I just couldn't, I just didn't listen to music for a little while after that tour, I was just so over that sound ... the heaviness ... the amount of bass that was coming through the stage ... six or seven gigs of the same lineup. And ... as the drums tech you've gotta sort of be there early in the day, pull it all out, set it all up making sure it's all right, and you've gotta kind of be there the whole time, you can't just run off and go and see some bands, [only to] come back and some of your drums are gone, that would be pretty bad. So yeah, that tour was fairly rough as far as being interested to music after that for a little while (James, age 41).

In James's mind, the continuous hum of heavy music backstage became unbearable, and without question, this kind of scenario is akin to working in an industrial environment. However, the objectionable sound that became so disturbing to James was tied directly to his passion (music), creating conflict in both the participant's career choice and leisure outlet. Unfortunately for James, this music still makes up part of his lifetime soundtrack because of its deleterious effect on his career.

The personal action of creating sounds can also create musical memories that are not fondly remembered, and even somewhat suppressed. Stella described how making mistakes on-stage became particularly poisonous in her memory:

> Yeah well, there used to a talent contest every year at my school and so, I used to enter every year, because I'm like, you know, a ham. So every year the song that I chose has remained – like I can barely listen to it now – 'cause I've got really awful memories of being really nervous and then usually failing somehow … Those songs are all ruined, permanently (Stella, age 22).

Negative reflection on performance anxiety and errors can be detrimental to the mental health of performers, whether the mistake was perceptible to the audience or not. As Stella mentions, the evasion of that music where possible is the best way to heal this trauma for her. This kind of experience with music is relatively unique to musicians and offers an alternative way of creating associations between music and daily events that persist in memory. These songs and their damaging link to performance and Stella's inner critic live on in her lifetime soundtrack.

Integrated musicality: Embodiment of music

When making music with an instrument or with the voice, musicians are interacting in specialized ways with their body and mind. Producing music involves various processes of internalizing and externalizing rhythm, meter, timbre, melody and harmony, which come from the relationship between musician and instrument. Nijs, Lesaffre and Leman describe this relationship as the "determining factor in the degree to which the musician's interaction with the musical environment is embodied" (2009: 138). Embodiment can take a number of forms, where an embodiment of music can be understood concurrently as comprehension and expression: a processing of information within the body and mind, and the physical use of the body to enact these learnings. This can include what is sometimes described as "kinaesthetic empathy" and includes gesture, facial expression and is usually nonverbal (Koivunen and Wennes 2011). In a 2006 article, van Dijck outlined her examination of online written responses to the annual "Dutch Top 2000" radio poll event. Interaction from listeners on the web resulted in aesthetic commentary as well as memory narratives; the latter of these were analysed by van Dijck who used these recollections to explore the relationship between personal and collective memory. As I've mentioned previously, the author contends that human memory is "simultaneously *embodied, enabled* and *embedded*" (2006: 358, emphasis original) and that this is particularly evident in musical memories. In her exploration of the topic, van Dijck emphasizes a mind-body connection – she views memories as being embodied in their creation through everyday routines; as enabled by listening technologies; and as embedded through the stimulation of memories in the present, bound by cultural contexts outside of the self.

Producing sound via an instrument or through voice typically engages the body through a coordinated set of movements that are at once creating and responding to sound. This is particularly important for professionals, who develop "corporeal capital" as they train their bodies to generate specific qualities (Gvion 2016). This physical activity is, in itself, a site of memory formation, where the action of music-making further embeds music into the psyche of a person. Cohen describes this as both a physical and spiritual connection; she observed UK musicians seeing "their instruments almost as an extension of themselves as a means through which to express their feelings" (1991: 190–91). Movement in making music is also explained through ideas of communicative gesture, where some movement that may not be necessary for the production of sound is used consciously by a performer for the benefit of the audience or other performers (see Davidson 2005).

This embodiment of music creates a pathway that is unique to musicians' memory and has particular effects on their lifetime soundtrack. James sees the physical side of his musicality interrupting everyday life:

> I mean … if I don't do a gig for a couple of weeks I start tapping a lot more, [my wife] notices it. She says, you've gotta go and do a gig because your fingers are "tap tap tap". So it's affecting me in that way, in that I'm thinking about it more obviously when I'm not playing (James, age 41).

Drumming not only relies on corporeal interaction with an instrument, it is also embedded in the idea of entrainment (discussed in Chapter 4), in which two autonomous rhythms synchronize, as when movements of the body synchronize with rhythms of music (Clayton, Sager and Will 2005). Drummer, Tony, recounted a set of narratives about his time playing in traditional music in a Greek venue:

> It made me realize that what was driving me was the intimacy of the relationship between me as a musician and the people, particularly people who were dancing, so it dawned on me that just by changing the intensity of how I played or the volume or how urgent or laid back I was compared to the pulse of the music, I could change the way large numbers of people responded, how they danced, make them dance more energetically, less energetically, more cohesively or less cohesively just by really subtle changes in how I played. And it dawned on me, this is a very intimate thing to do, you're tampering with people's sort of emotions, but it's on a large number of people, and nobody would know what I was doing (Tony, age 62).

In this experience, Tony is leading the tempo of the band but is also learning about the nature of entrainment between dancers and music. Changes in his playing had very subtle but highly responsive effects on those around him. Tony described this as particularly instructive, developing his understanding of musicianship on a higher level.

Experiences of music-making such as this might align with concepts raised by aforementioned scholars Nijs, Lesaffre and Leman (2009: 3), who describe a "merging" of body and instrument, where the technical demands of the instrument become so coordinated into human movement they become "transparent". This allows the musician to respond to their musical environment in direct ways, unhindered by thoughts relating to sound production. Tony recalled a number of instances playing in this band in which he was acutely aware of a somewhat transcendental state of mind while performing. He describes his early style of playing as "very analytical and precise and mathematical"; however, this was to change suddenly one evening:

> It happened by accident one night … all of a sudden there was a complicated thing, seven-four time signature, complex, difficult arrangements, anyway, something happened and I lost track of where I was, but I kept playing because you never stopped – rule one, never stop until everyone else does. And much to my amazement everything kept coming out fine and I had no intellectual connection whatsoever, I was just sitting there, the music was coming out and it was sort of like an out of body experience in the sense that I was listening and observing what was happening, but I was no longer in control of it (Tony, age 62).

What Tony is experiencing in this recollection aligns with a concept referred to as "flow". The idea of flow as a state of consciousness has been extensively investigated by Mihaly Csikszentmihalyi, who describes it as "a state of optimal experience that people report when they are intensely involved in something that is fun to do" (2000: 381). "Flow" can occur in many professions or activities and requires total immersion in the activity such that one is in a state of focused absorption (Bloom and Skutnick-Henley 2005). It is often incorporated into deep performative musical experiences, like the one Tony describes. Csikszentmihalyi (1997) was the first to define the characteristics of "flow", several of which are present in Tony's experience, including: a distortion of one's sense of time, a feeling that the activity is intrinsically rewarding, immediate feedback from the self, and ostensibly, an exclusion of extraneous material from conscious thought. In his narration Tony describes feeling a loss of control, and though this calm sensation may seem to align with the idea of flow, this is actually an element that is contrary to Csikszentmihalyi's definition. However, in the performative context of this occurrence, such a notion could be attributed to the state of musician-instrument connection as described by Nijs and colleagues (2009) above, which is usually only achieved through a state of flow.

Flow in practice and performance relies on an alignment of internal and external factors, and scholarship has yet to reveal how common musical states of flow truly are. There are other examples of how musical embodiment or, moreover, some representation of this, can come about in more subtle ways, especially in relation to emotion and personal perception. In Matthew's narrative below, he describes how a series of events regarding his performance affected the kinds of music he wanted to play, which he in turn embodied:

> Go back to third year of uni, second semester, I got really, really horrible marks for my playing exam, which I was really upset about because that was the first playing exam I thought I played well on ... I started fourth year listening to a lot more aggressive sort of really, really aggressive jazz ... Relatively, I guess [those songs are] very important ... they sort of signify the strength of self that I learned in that year which was ah sort of bizarre. I guess a lot of people always associate me with being very loud and noisy and but it was a lot of introspective thought that came even before that ... for that year those were the tunes that inspired a lot of the deeper thought I guess, from that year (Matthew, age 25).

The signification of a "strength of self" is at the focal point of this story. Matthew was using music as a means of expression, which works on two levels for him as a musician: he can both play the music as expression, and simultaneously hear and validate this in the music, whether listening to himself, or recorded versions. In some ways, Matthew is managing his emotions, but in a contrasting way than previously discussed – this example is purposeful, signifying an attempt to channel, if not control, his own emotion through music-making.

One final thought on the profound ways music may affect musicians leads us back to Tony, whose spiritual connection with music expressed itself in an unexpected way. As established in Chapter 2, the lifetime soundtrack is often influenced by parents' or caregivers' musical preferences. Typically, this occurs through recorded music, but it is also the case with music that is sung or performed around children. Tony describes his experience of his father's musical performances as a child:

> When I was a little kid ... if you were very good you were allowed to go to gigs, so my Dad for example was the bandleader at "Cloudland"[5] for a time, and I have extremely good memories of when we were very, very good, and me and my sister were allowed to go, in our pyjamas, and we'd go up to the balcony which was rarely opened in those days, and peer over the balcony, watch everybody dancing and watch Dad playing. And one of the big songs for a drummer in those days was 'Golden Wedding'.[6] It's a drum solo, drum and clarinet sort of solo piece, done by Benny Goodman I think. So that song, whenever I heard that song I'm reminded, whenever I play that song it reminds me a lot of my Dad. And ... if I was playing swing music, I mean, doing it well, if everything was gelling, I could sort of feel his presence, and it was nearly like I was channelling him when I played in that style (Tony, age 62).

This narrative is striking because of the temporal connections that are being made between visual, aural and tactile experiences as a child, and musical abilities realized some time later, thereby encompassing roles on a continuum from audience member to performer. Further, the mnemonic association between these experiences and the music is based in its performance, specifically as a drummer. The memory of seeing his father play is a long-lasting one, considering this is one of Tony's very earliest memories, which indicates it is particularly meaningful for Tony, and was perhaps enhanced when he first experienced this intangible, spiritual connection when playing. Certainly, the initial experience may have been instructive for a young Tony, yet to really begin his own music journey, which aligns with Sloboda's thoughts on the positive influence of "peak emotional experiences" on long-term engagement with music (1991). This last story of Tony's is a particularly good example of the purpose of this chapter – which was to display the attributes of musical memory as it sometimes plays out for musicians. To feel, hear and see things a little differently because of musical training can mean that one remembers, associates and recalls some musical memory events in alternate ways.

Conclusion

This chapter has outlined some of the ways in which participation in music-making, whether as a casual, self-taught hobbyist or working professionally as a musician, might influence the kinds of experiences embedded in the lifetime soundtrack. This can be through a greater depth of knowledge on how music is composed, produced or recorded, which can in turn guide the interpretation of recorded or live music, and affect the way music is remembered. The practice of music, in any form, can inform the development of personal identity in ways that are less frequently encountered by people who do not sing or play an instrument. The effects of emotional labour sometimes felt by professional musicians can alter the relationship a performer might have with music, enabling them to work with the demands of repetitious or otherwise personally draining circumstances. So, while an audience may take a memory away from a recording or show that is personal or significant to them, the contexts of that memory will almost certainly be different for the performer. This dichotomy highlights differences in perception between these two agents on opposing sides of the stage as relative to their experience, both in the moment and over time. I return to the work of van Dijck (2006), who, in describing musical memory as embodied, perhaps did not consider how that might play out for musicians, whose minds and bodies are so literally part of the process of musical embodiment. This is something that is shared by amateur and professional musicians alike – the feel and response of an instrument against the body, or within the body in the case of the voice, brings the ultimate tactile sense to musical memories. The lifetime soundtrack can be both broadened and hindered by music participation. On the one side, music-making increases the diversity of sensations, interactions and mind-sets that help to create musical memories, yet, on the other, not all experiences rehearsing, producing and performing music are instructive or integral to one's sense of self, nor affect the overall level of meaning that reflexive practices with music can reveal.

Notes

1. A school in Brisbane, Queensland, Australia.
2. A live music venue in Brisbane, popular in the 1990s.
3. Common anti-inflammatory medication.
4. A jazz standard by Weiss/Douglas, made famous by Louis Armstrong in 1967.
5. "Cloudland" was an entertainment venue and ballroom, which opened in Brisbane, Australia in 1940, and was controversially demolished in 1982.
6. Made famous by Woody Herman.

6   Change: The Past, Present and Future of the Lifetime Soundtrack

> Rather than being isolated operations of minds or brains (or of isolated cellular, molecular, or cognitive systems of these brains), these practices [of remembering and forgetting] are carried out by people. That is, they are realized by persons with agency, intentionality, and the brain states that entail and enable such agency and intentionality. In other words, human memory practices are embedded or embodied – in environments, *umwelt*s, eco-niches, everyday life-meaning contexts, and historical lifeworlds of action and interaction; they are activities within cultural (and that implies noetic) orders, which are themselves subject to historical change (Brockmeier 2010: 27).

Change can occur in many forms. In the context of music listening practices, it can be a natural human change, like maturity of mind and ageing of the body, or influenced by external factors, such as new music trends or technologies. Our attitude to music may change, or the meaning of memories we associate with music can transform, as we come across new people, places and experiences. The lifetime soundtrack is continually modulating in reaction to the present moment, aligning with Brockmeier's ideas on memory, above. Some musical memories may become less important and become diminished in strength or forgotten altogether; other parts of the lifetime soundtrack may be reinforced as significant and retain their standing over time. Personal taste and the influence of people around us are likely to vary over time; however, a preference for listening to music from our youth can arguably slow the addition of new music to our personal soundtrack. This chapter allows for a deeper and more theoretical exploration of the lifetime soundtrack as it develops over time. It presents alternative ways in which people may add to their lifetime soundtrack or come to understand it. Though it is not the only factor at play, the notion of change is a useful lens through which to view the process of canonization – remembering and forgetting – that shapes the lifetime soundtrack. Some discussion points in this chapter have been mentioned in other parts of this book, usually in passing. Here, special attention is paid to concepts such as ageing and mortality, commemorative music, reflexive use of music, nostalgia, emotion, and meaning-making in relation to change and the lifetime soundtrack.

Canonization and retrospect: Remembering and forgetting

Earlier in this book, the music encountered in childhood and adolescence was established as instructive in the foundation of the lifetime soundtrack. The life stage of adolescence brings with it a host of new experiences that can significantly influence the lifetime soundtrack and autobiographical memory, but it is also a period of focus for memory researchers because it is during adolescence that we develop certain elements of maturity regarding memory. Bluck and Habermas (2001; Habermas and Bluck 2000) note that adolescence is critical for the development of a cognitive process used in reminiscing, which they call "autobiographical reasoning". The authors define this process as one of "self-reflective thinking or talking about the personal past that involves forming links between elements of one's life and the self in an attempt to relate one's personal past and present" (2001: 136). Such a skill is echoed in the earlier definition of autobiographical memory given by Fivush (2011), which described the requirement for reflection and evaluation of experiences through the use of perspective. The latter element is most notably missing from adolescents' memory narratives due to their inability to temporally distance themselves from experiences. Autobiographical reasoning helps to develop a narrative identity which continues to be maintained and refreshed for the rest of one's life (McAdams 2008). The autobiographical stories we tell ourselves continue to be remodelled to make sense of life at any one time, to make a coherent account of our experiences. Sometimes life events make sense immediately in the context of those that have gone before; however, others may require some time and perspective to find their way into our life story. This is significant for the lifetime soundtrack, as it is through the acquisition and application of autobiographical reasoning that the soundtrack can begin to take on a more permanent shape, which I propose occurs through processes of remembering and forgetting referred to here as *canonization*.

The concept of canonization has been raised throughout this book, because it is constantly at play: whenever we reflect on our musical memories, newer additions are compared to older experiences and vice versa, competing for space in our minds. The notion of retrospective evaluation of musical memories has also cropped up within the previous chapters, especially when participants are able to tell what are now "whole" stories, where gaps and rationales for emotional responses have been subsequently resolved. Canonization itself represents a form of internal change that is happening concurrently as our sound environment and other factors out of our control begin to shift over time. The need to wait for the passage of time to smooth over memories is something that is part of this pattern of remembering and forgetting. Notably, few interviewees spoke of very recent events; even those who were young adults seemed to need temporal distance from their freshest memories to determine their significance. For the most part, this book has looked to the direct connection of music and memory in one moment to explore the lifetime soundtrack: these were the most common type of narratives given by participants. Some narratives, however, suggest that music has become associated with memories in retrospect, emphasizing the role of time and retrospect in the processes of canonization. In Riley's story, below, he describes competing situations that could all have become associated with music from the *Top Gun* soundtrack, but one scenario only becomes the key memory:

> [In] South Africa I listened to a mix of music, I just had my iPod on shuffle the entire time … apart from the *Top Gun* soundtrack … We travelled up the coast with a guy I worked with and we just listened to the *Top Gun* soundtrack on loops. So now I can't help but think, even though I've listened to so much *Top Gun* at university, I feel it should remind me of that – but it doesn't, it reminds me of that trip. Because I watched a lot of it, and we used to play the soundtrack a lot, but it actually reminds me of that trip, not university, when I used to watch *Top Gun* three times a day (Riley, age 26).

The link between either event or set of events and the soundtrack was probably not made at the time. It is only in retrospect that Riley can recognize which is the stronger, or more important, association. In another example, Ian details a connection between a memory and music that was not present at the same time:

> 'The Swiss Maid', by Del Shannon … The man who owned the farm [my family worked on], he died in a car accident and then the Kranstons came, and this song was about that time. I remember standing on the back of a truck and um, we had to go to Kimbolton which is about 20 kilometres away from where we lived on the farm. I remember we went there, we went on the back of a truck, and I was sitting on the back of the truck, and I don't know, that reminds me of it. I think it reminds me of it because it was, because I used to listen to this song a lot and it's all about you know this guy's frustrated love, and um, and it was all about, "on a mountain" and that sort of thing. I think I really remember it now because you know we had to drive right near Kimbolton, where we lived was on the plains but just a little bit further out was on the hills and that sort of thing (Ian, age 60).

This song is one that Ian says he used to listen to a lot – probably around the time of the activities that he is recounting. However, the song doesn't seem to be playing from the truck while Ian is taking in the scenery, travelling around his home town. Here, a few *sticky* parts of memory seem to have come together over time. As a cloud memory, Ian remembers listening to 'The Swiss Maid' over a period of weeks or months, with no one specific memory from which he is hearing it. Instead, he has made associations, in retrospect, between the song and this snapshot from his young life both because of the temporal commonality and because of the song's descriptions of landscapes which fit with his visual memory of the area. Stories such as those of Ian and Riley go some way to explaining how the lifetime soundtrack continues to develop in a number of ways as we age. Not only do we add new music, extending the breadth of the soundtrack, but we also go back, not always purposefully, to better understand our experiences. In so doing, we expand the soundtrack's depth, creating new meanings through the processes of retrospect and canonization.

Ageing, music taste and consumption

Changes in the body and mind are inevitable as we grow and age. Already, this book has established that music perception and memory formation are processes that develop from infancy, through adolescence and beyond. In contrast, emerging work in music sociology and psychology has turned to the patterns of music taste and consumption in older people, which collectively signal differences between the way older and younger people interact with music. Anecdotally, older people prefer to listen to music that was popular or important to them when they were coming of age – in adolescence and young adulthood. This is evidenced in the nostalgic production of media for older people (Kusumi, Matsuda and Sugimori 2010), such as radio, television and music releases, and is further promoted by discourses of ageing in popular culture. Whether this is accurate or mythologized is debatable; as times change, the generational split regarding music preferences diminishes (Connell 2012) and older people continue to employ music to signify personal identity (Hays and Minichiello 2005; Bennett and Hodkinson 2012), drawing largely on their lifetime soundtrack. Though Harrison and Ryan (2010) believe that cultural taste narrows in old age due to a reduced need for cultural capital, more recent research argues many older people are keen to keep up with modern music trends (Forman 2012). However, many participants in my research maintained a preference for music from their youth, with narratives relating to adolescence dominating their soundtrack, followed by childhood and young adulthood. As music psychologists have shown, music from one's youth often remains significant due to its integration with new and formative experiences (e.g. Baumgartner 1992), but this does not necessarily preclude people from maintaining an interest in new music over time.

These arguments aside, taste – as pointed out several times already – is not the sole source of the lifetime soundtrack, though preferences do tend to guide music that dominates it. Nonetheless, reflexive memory practices are more likely to occur in response to music that one likes, particularly if the ability exists to replay that music on current technologies. In the most traditional sense, reflexive practice in old age often engages with nostalgia and feelings related to reminiscence. In Chapter 4, I referred to an idea that memory – particularly musical memory – that is pushed far enough back in time can be stored in a metaphorical vault. The memory vault requires triggers to open, such that hearing salient music invites a flood of images, feelings, scents and thoughts. Perhaps, in the context of change, the potential arises for external trends to further consolidate the memory vault. As music progresses within and beyond genre boundaries, the sounds, lyrics and cultures that we have associated with our memories become more diverse, or at least, further contrasted with the music we once loved. At the same time, advancements in listening technologies can alter the aesthetics and accessibility of listening – from the actions of setting up the device (e.g. aligning the needle on a turntable) to the quality of sound. I suggest that the packing away of music genres and patterns of consumption that comes with the induction of newer genres and styles further enforces the seal of the memory vault, by distancing fans from the original contexts of music experience.

Susan, below, spoke about the importance of music being linked to the intensity with which she listened:

> Oh I think [music has] been extremely important, it's been very important all through my life, but I think those years of adolescence, probably was when music was the most, hmm, I well and truly would sit for hours, *all* afternoon, hours, and lost myself in the music for like four or five hours at a time. So, at a very painful time, it was I think it would have been the most intense ... when I was getting separated. I used it a lot and I listened to it a lot, intensely, but probably not for four or five hours at a time because as an adult I'm much more complex ... as that adolescent I really ... was still shaping myself as a person and I ... was still feeling that, looseness ... when I was a kid, I felt, "it's not ready yet, I'm not cooked yet" (Susan, age 52).

The years of adolescence are accentuated here; often due to lack of responsibilities or commitments, and the popularity of music as a pastime for teenagers, a great deal of time can be spent just listening and doing little else. As described in other chapters, Susan reached out for the comfort of music that seemed to be articulating her emotional pain during her divorce, but she was still unable to replicate the length of time spent listening to music in her youth. What Susan also refers to in her narrative is a feeling of incompleteness as a teen, of growing still left to do. This is an astute insight that can be, in a slightly abstract way, brought back to the development of identity and the recurrent reflexive practices that occur in coming to terms with who one is or wants to be, often to the backdrop of music (Tarrant, North and Hargreaves 2002). As we experience mature adulthood and what follows, listening habits and reasons for engaging with music may find new ways of manifesting or may decrease due to a lack of free time, contrasting with times of deep or excessive want or need for music. When I asked Vincent if his engagement with music had varied over his life, he said:

> One of the things you will probably find about yourself in time, is the capacity to experience a certain range of feelings, attitudes, experiences is greater than other times. You don't have time for it, cos of worries, pressures, whatever. Life is like a switchback you know, you come along, you have a period of tranquillity and then – brrrr! – it's one of those things that's head down tail up, you've haven't got time to think. And in the middle of rearing family, especially when you've got four of them, it's which crisis is going to happen tomorrow, what's going to happen on Thursday. Can you make an appointment for one week out and give yourself a bit of time to prepare for it? You wish. Those sort of things happen (Vincent, age 77).

Vincent lists "feelings, attitudes, experiences" as things that mature adult life sometimes does not leave time for. We can potentially add to this list reflexive practices, particularly with music, when there may be less time available for bouts of listening and thinking about the meaning of particular music in the context of our lives.

Projected memory: Commemorating the self and preparing for change

Connections between the lifetime soundtrack, the life story and personal identity often benefit from retrospection, when subsequent experiences, knowledge and changes in attitude can be applied to explain meaning and significance. However, some critical points of realization about the future of this relationship appeared when interviewees were thinking reflexively about the role of music in their lives so far, and the way they might choose to integrate music in the remainder of their lives. As such, a notion of *projected (musical) memory* is applied to these thoughts to help conceptualize the ways in which we think about ideal events or circumstances that we hope will befall us in the near and distant futures of our lives. One way in which this idealized projection presented itself in interviews was through the prediction of major events and the use of music therein, including one's own funeral service, which we can view in the current context as planning for change. Unruh (1983) provides a useful way for thinking about how music, identity and the end of life come together through his theories of identity preservation activities. Unruh describes that, as a person comes toward the end of their life, they begin to consolidate their identity through the gathering and sometimes distribution of "artefacts" or other symbols that represent themselves in the way they would like to be remembered. Music could be considered as one way in which the departed can be memorialized, taking the form of an intangible artefact of identity (Holloway *et al.* 2013; Howarth 2000).

Earlier, the connection between music, emotion and music selected for funerals was discussed in reference to the experience of the living, who described the kinds of music that now are bonded to strong affective memories. Unexpectedly, some other interviewees projected the music they would like played at their own funeral, often because they thought the music may represent their identity, spirit or experiences holistically. Unruh describes this activity taking place towards the end of life; however, some participant narratives indicate initial thoughts on the selection of musical identity artefacts could occur much earlier:

> I know one song that I want played for sure, and I've made sure that [my wife] knows what it is: 'Paradise City' by Guns N' Roses. And I've actually just been thinking a bit about it lately, but yeah that's the only one that I know for sure. I've thought about it but nothing's made the list as a definite yet other than 'Paradise City', but yeah I've been thinking about making a list soon (Jeremy, age 36).

Throughout his interview Jeremy had described an obsession with Guns N' Roses that had captivated him since first hearing their music in adolescence. Although Jeremy has a love for many other genres of music, and has avidly followed other bands, it seems that his connection with Guns N' Roses arises clearly as part of the memory he wishes to leave behind in others. A musical legacy like this sees the spirit of the deceased "continuing in memory" (Holloway *et al.* 2013). The authors note the difference between this concept and "remembering" is the implication of a continuing relationship, which in this case is via a musical connection.

Instances where individuals pre-selected music for a future event contrast with the majority of memory and music interactions represented here, because these are circumstances that are hoped for, but have not yet been realized. Nonetheless, a rather significant process in memory work is taking place when these thoughts arise. Though these aren't technically memories, in terms of their temporal position in lived experience, they *are* a result of reflexive thinking on autobiographical experience. In research focused on funeral music selection in the UK, Adamson and Holloway state music in the contexts of funerals is a "central element in the complex process of seeking, creating, and taking of meaning" (2012: 45).

This may be the case for those experiencing the ceremony; however, this meaning-making process could also be undertaken before death through the pre-selection of music for one's own funeral, especially that music which could aid loved ones in the grieving process. In listening to music and thinking about its meaning, the imagination becomes engaged not only in reflecting on life (as in Keightley and Pickering's "mnemonic imagination", 2012), but also in imagining one's prospects. In pre-selecting music for one's own funeral, the individual is choosing to communicate something about themselves to their audience. Within this setting, this action takes on a special significance, as a legacy or communicative symbol to be interpreted by the living.

Letting loved ones know about preferences for funeral music is an essential step taken by Ian, who has held an affinity with Jimi Hendrix's music from an early age:

> [Speaking of 'Voodoo Chile (Slight Return)' by Jimi Hendrix] This is my all-time favourite. I said to [my daughter], they can play this at my funeral ... He was so good. I mean, this was just genius. And I always congratulate myself because I was the one who told everyone about Jimi Hendrix at school. I was the one who found Jimi Hendrix, and no one else was listening to Jimi Hendrix and I told them all about Jimi Hendrix (Ian, age 60).

Here, it would seem that this music is significant not only on the level of aural enjoyment, but also due to its significance in Ian's social development and maturity in musical taste. This anecdote almost serves as a metaphor for Ian's interaction with music over his lifetime: Ian mused that he often felt at the forefront of new music trends among his peers, especially during the 50s, 60s and 70s. Music has clearly been significant to Ian throughout his life; in choosing this Jimi Hendrix song, it seems he is selecting something that is the pinnacle of this aspect of his identity, and therefore, in the context of a funeral, the music portrays a substantive part of this to others.

For Paul, however, there were other reasons for his choice of funeral music. The interview excerpt below recounts his selection process:

> *Paul:* So this is a song called 'New Grass' by Talk Talk and it's one of those songs that I still don't know what it means, I can barely hear the lyrics, all of the pieces of music don't quite fit together even though it's still quite melodic ... yeah, I mean that's the sort of music, one of those two songs [the other song being 'Weightlifting' by The Trash Can Sinatras] I'd like to have played at my funeral, that would be quite nice.

> *Interviewer:* For what reasons have you picked those songs?

Paul: Uh I have mused that … I've thought about the fact that particularly that Talk Talk song 'New Grass' is long, it's beautiful and I don't really know what it means, and think that's a little bit like life itself really, you just have to experience it, or something. I mean, that's going to sound really tacky to write it down.

Interviewer: Were you hoping for a certain reaction if that song is played at your funeral, were you thinking about what other people's reactions might be?

Paul: It's very egotistical isn't it? Um, no, just a certain kind of stillness and, a stillness and suspension maybe, for a longer period than one might ordinarily expect to listen to pop music or something like that, maybe that would be it, just want that feeling of stillness and suspension (Paul, age 42).

The process of identifying just one or two pieces of music that somehow reflect one's personality, values or journey through life requires reflection on the lifetime soundtrack and its parallel flow with the life story. For Paul, his musical choice seems to be a broad metaphor for his experience and life in general; he also considers the function of the song within the ceremony as part of his rationale. This selection more abstractly represents Paul's identity, compared to Ian or Jeremy, as Paul is thinking a little more broadly about the aesthetic of the music, and the resonance that it might evoke. This is something that Paul wants to leave with others, sharing some element of his life experience by creating a moment "of suspension" for others. Nonetheless, his experience with this music and his choosing of it for a self-commemorating ceremony suggests 'New Grass' is closely tied to Paul's narrative identity. In all of the above examples, the music has been chosen in the first instance because it is significant for the individual and they envisage it retaining this importance throughout their lifetime, thereby constituting an artefact of the self. It has also been chosen to engender specific feelings in the listeners.

The projection of memory onto other life events also included thoughts about weddings. Similar to music being used in funerals, wedding music, in Western countries at least, has become increasingly personalized and secularized, probably owing, in part, to the increased use of celebrants to officiate marriages and the breakdown of religious authority in Western postmodern society (Quinlan 2016). Anecdotally, the wedding day remains a significant reference point for an individual throughout their life, and the role of music in facilitating mood and affect both at the time, and in remembrance, is significant. Very few people interviewed for this book described their wedding day, despite more than half of them experiencing marriage at some point; as discussed in Chapter 3, people were more inclined to talk about musical associations with ex-lovers. Only one participant (married once, now divorced) recounted a trigger for memories of her wedding:

> My brother in law drove the wedding car to the church when I was getting married and he had playing in the car 'You are So Beautiful' by Joe Cocker, and every time I hear that it takes me back to that car every single time, I'm sitting back in the car in my wedding dress. So, there's that one, and on that same day we had 'Can I Have This Dance for the Rest of My Life' by Anne Murray, same thing, taken back to dancing at my wedding (Robyn, age 52).

These two songs are very strongly connected to this special experience for Robyn. Despite the marriage in this memory later ending in divorce, the participant retains positive memories of the event via song. In intriguing cases, some participants who were not yet married had already made some choices towards music they want played at their own wedding ceremony. Though there isn't as much of a need to gather this music as an artefact of the self, as in preparation for dying, the modern understanding that music selected for one's wedding will remain personally significant creates a desire to select the "perfect" music.

In contrast to funeral music that often represents just one person, music for a wedding ceremony would, ostensibly, represent two people or the relationship as a whole. Paul, who above described his anticipated funeral, went on to speak about his outlook on music for his own wedding:

> And there's a particular joyous piece of music called 'You are the Best Thing' by an artist called Ray Lamontagne, and I thought that would be a brilliant walking down the aisle song with my partner, 'cause we haven't got married yet. So that's a slightly more joyous thing I've thought, if there were a soundtrack to my wedding that would be the walking down the aisle tune ... It's a very joyous piece of music, it's almost too obvious so it's ... good-spiritedly ironic, in its ceremonial use in my mind, like you know we've experienced something more stately but it's really a party song (Paul, age 42).

Paul has thought carefully about how this music might symbolize the emotion of the ceremony, by capturing both the serious and celebratory sections of the day. It is also likely that Paul has his partner in mind, given the direct, positive lyrical message of the song. As with the funeral music choices, participants like Paul are projecting memories based on their past experiences. The emotional sentiment of music chosen for such an event is also important to this participant, who describes his choice as a "very joyous" one. Stella also has definite ideas about her choice of wedding music:

> I would want the Eric Whitacre song 'A Boy and a Girl' that I lis-
> tened to [when I was travelling] in Africa. I want that! (Speaks
> louder so her partner in the next room might hear:) "That's all I
> know that I want, I want that at my wedding, I desperately want
> that. Whoever it may be. Anyone. Anyone who would." I would
> have that there. That would mean something to me. It's like a little
> love song but not in a cheesy way. I think that would mean some-
> thing to me. I know it does, that's why I want it (Stella, age 22).

Stella emphasizes the part that music would play in adding meaning to this
occasion, such that the music would communicate an emotional message to
those in attendance, as well as fulfilling her own desires. In this instance,
the music does not appear to be quite as significant to her partner: Stella
travelled through Africa on a family holiday without her boyfriend, and so
she is bringing her own strong associations into the equation. At the same
time, because it is a piece of music that is important to her, it is likely she
has shared this music with others, especially her partner, as part of her
identity.

Several similarities have been drawn between the pre-selection of funeral
music and the planning of wedding music; however there is one significant
difference between these two events which lies in the experience of the individual. Both events present an opportunity to create memories for those in
attendance; such is the intent behind pre-selecting music that is personally
meaningful. In the case of a wedding, the bride and/or groom choose music,
and then are able to experience and subsequently memorialize the music, the
activities and the emotions that accompany it. They choose certain music
because they purposefully wish to make associations between the event and
the music: an association that will remain in their lifetime soundtrack. In the
case of a funeral, however, the individual will not be present to make memories of the occasion. The music choice in this instance then offers a sense of
conclusiveness, a last message, and a final chance to make a mnemonic connection between music and significant others.

Corporeal change: The body and ageing

While commemorating the self in preparation for a foreseen change involves
introspective processes, change can also come in physical forms that affect the
mind and body in different ways. With ageing comes the inevitable processes
that modify the ways in which our bodies perceive and react to music. Physically and mentally, it is likely that limitations including hearing loss, fatigue,
limitations to mobility and coordination, semantic memory loss, identity,
and agency, will affect us all to some degree. The relationship each individual
has with music may undergo some alteration, in terms of how they interact
with it; listening, singing, or playing an instrument are all activities that may

be affected by the afflictions of age. Though this research did not set out to attend to the question of how this plays out, it was nonetheless encountered both in interview narratives, and within the situational context of some interviews. The effects of ageing were noted most prominently by two musicians, and it is to these individuals I now turn.

While some attention has been given to ageing rock stars and the now ageing communities of youth subcultures (Jennings and Gardner 2012; Hodkinson and Bennett and Hodkinson 2012; Bennett 2013), less is known about the ways ageing affects working and amateur musicians. The physicality that is involved in the creation of music is empowering for the able-bodied musician. The regular challenges of ageing can affect musicians in critical ways that might prevent them playing or singing and interacting with other musicians in the ways they used to (see for example Barton 2004). Such effects can be brought on by the independent ageing process, but also as a compounded problem arising from the occupational hazards of music-making, for example accelerated hearing loss through work in orchestras or rock bands (Emmerich, Rudel and Richter 2008; Palin 1994). Although some research has shown that continued participation in musical activities in older life phases can be important for social and mental well-being (e.g. Gembris 2008), these activities require an aspect of negotiation. Two of the small group of musicians who took part in interviews also articulated the ways ageing has affected them. Their stories serve as examples of the ways ageing can shape the lifetime soundtrack, especially in later life.

Ron, age 59

Ron has participated in music for most of his adult life; he plays trumpet in community bands and is an avid listener with a vast collection of jazz music at his fingertips. Approaching 60 years of age at the time of interview, Ron tells of his frustration with the passing of time:

> I've even got to the stage where it becomes so frustrating because it's encompassing, that you think of giving it away. Probably in the last five to ten years I've seriously thought about it five to ten times of tossing it in altogether and trying to find another hobby or something like that that wasn't so demanding mentally and physically because I also play, see?

Ron goes on further in the interview to explain that he feels that in order to become a better musician he not only needs to perform in bands and consistently practise his instrument, but also goes out to see live music. With all three types of activities occurring on both weeknights and weekends around Ron's day job, there is not much time left over for high-level development on his instrument. Impediments to mobility, including walking and driving, impact on the agency of an individual, but also the social aspect that comes with attending rehearsals and live music gigs.

Ron is frustrated by his slowing ability to keep up with what he feels is required, and the awareness of declining capacity shapes his autobiographical reflections. He says that several aspects of his playing had begun to improve recently, through a new attitude towards practice and a way of thinking about music in general. This unfortunately only compounds his irritation:

> I wish I'd known that when I was 20 because I'd have another ten years to perfect it and the rest of my musical life to do it, whereas now it's – you're almost looking at the downhill side. When you're 60 you haven't got that many years, but we'll see what happens. A burden is what I'd put it at.

Despite the drive that Ron has had to pursue music for so long, the feeling of never reaching the pinnacle of experience, shackled by the responsibilities of adult life, has left Ron feeling despondent and resentful about his experiences. Added to this is the degree to which music is part of his identity: although he threatens himself with giving up music completely, it is far too significant in terms of personal identity to be removed altogether from his lifestyle. While Ron's ideas of music as a "burden" throughout life may not be shared by all ageing musicians, the physical and mental demands of music practice are bound to be affected in some ways by changes associated with ageing.

Bea, age 81

As a vocalist in her twenties, Bea found herself swept up into family life but never lost her passion for music. In our interview, Bea told of the great deal of loss she had suffered in the years previous, and the intensity with which they had become associated with music. She listens to the radio, and sings, but avoids engaging with some recorded music, perhaps because it is too strong a reminder of her husband and son.

> But if you are a singer, you do sing, you sing along with the music and things like this ... but you can also sing within your head, have you noticed you can do that? So I get up and I have a little [sing], because I do suffer a little bit with the blues, I think because I wear my heart too much on my sleeve, but that's the nature of the person, I can't change, that's just me.

As Bea points out, some things about a person *don't* change over time; she will always retain core affective parts of her personality and identity:

> I had two sisters, and they used to always laugh at me and they'd say, "There's [Bea] in her rose-coloured world" and I think if you're a singer you do live in a rose-coloured world. A rose-coloured world, yes. They've always said that to me. And you do. So, think about that.

Bea also talks about how singing makes her feel, despite the limitations ageing has placed on her voice:

> Um, you feel a happiness within yourself when you sing, and even if you don't, if I don't sing, I can't sing now the old voice is gone, which it does, and the older you get, the tremor upsets the voice now, but when you sing in your head you don't hear it, you don't hear the tremor. You sound as you were (Bea, age 81).

Not being able to play an instrument as well as before, or even at all, can have an enormous impact on a person's sense of self. In such cases, it is also possible that person might also lose a sense of their purpose in life, compounded by other factors of older age. Nonetheless, being able to imagine the sound of a younger self is helpful for Bea, who uses her inner voice to engage in memories that bring her happiness but also act as affirmation to her life experiences, both joyous and sorrowful. What both Bea and Ron are describing is the way that changes in their life, physical and mental, have changed the way they interact with music as musicians, which in turn can affect the way they attune to their musical memories and lifetime soundtrack.

Meaning-making: Change and stability

In reviewing how the lifetime soundtrack is influenced over time, one of the most striking features I've found is probably also one of the most subtle and personal. Though participants told stories about the lifetime soundtrack as they perceived them at that present moment within the interview, there was at times a suggestion that some music had changed in its meaning or importance. Being slightly more difficult to capture in memory narratives, the processes of change that occur internally and externally may in turn alter the way we feel about certain music, not just because of transformations in taste (though this is not without effect), but because of a growing assemblage of experiences. The natural shift in attitudes and perceptions that we will develop over time inform the ongoing process of lifetime soundtrack canonization. This ebb and flow of memory and meaning occurs within a framework of constants: there are some memories that will maintain significance over time and may become the cornerstones around which more short-term alliances with musical memories (and relationships with people, places and things more broadly) revolve.

Of the memory narratives I collected, the most volatile change of meaning was for those associated with romantic relationships, or with situations that now cause negative feelings. Stories examined in Chapter 3 highlighted the frequent use of music in forming relationships and the prevalence of "our song", i.e. music that people associate with a relationship. In instances such as Angela's description of 'River' by Joni Mitchell ("I love it now to listen to it, but if I listen to it I'm feeling a bit sad") or Bea's refusal to play music she used to enjoy with her late husband ("I haven't played my tapes since I lost Nelson"), it is not the connection between the music and the relationship that has changed, but their perception of the music at the present time. In another example, Susan's narrative linking a particular Foo Fighters album with her marriage break-up demonstrates a longing for change:

> I love the album, but I played it a lot when my marriage was breaking up. And now when I play it I feel so horrible and sad inside that I um, I'd like to get rid of that, I'd like to undo that connection 'cause I really love it (Susan, age 52).

Like Angela, Susan still has a liking for the music itself, signalling that taste here is more stable but that harsh emotional association stands in the way of full enjoyment. Though relationships are perhaps one of the more common reasons for the meaning of music and associated memories to transform, this need not be the only one. More subtle changes in maturity guided by new life experiences, or even repeated ones, can influence the perception of the lifetime soundtrack. In retrospect, most memory narratives presented in this book may have undergone some kind of change not articulated by interviewees and may have changed meaning again since they were originally recounted to me.

Despite the necessity of change in the lifetime soundtrack, there is also a contrasting stability. Once canonized, some musical memories remain more or less static; they are foundational to the identity of a person and are likely to remain so for a good deal of time. The fact that music of one's youth often retains its place as a preferred music for many people, and the likelihood that this music will evoke nostalgic thoughts, has not been overlooked by the music industry. Since the 1980s, rock and pop music from the 1960s and 70s is increasingly republished, re-toured and replicated, likely due to a growing audience of baby-boomers with renewed levels of disposable income (Bennett 2009, see also Homan 2006). This generation was the first to experience popular music, which grew with them as they entered adolescence and young adulthood. By extension, then, they are the first to experience an attachment between popular music and their sense of self, which has particular impact in terms of music sociology and the creation of modern subcultures. Though the lifetime soundtrack is rarely exclusively made out of popular music, there are clear links between identity, music and the lifetime soundtrack as pointed out in other parts of this book.

My argument, however, is that music, especially popular music, that has become a stable, meaningful part of lifetime soundtracks around the world, can be, and has been, capitalized upon by various sectors of the modern music industry. This idea has been touched on by a range of scholars who have noticed the surge in heritage rock, a concept raised most prominently by Bennett (2009). Originally characterized through reference to the *Classic Albums Live* concert series, Bennett describes heritage rock as reinforcing a music canon already "endorsed" by mainstream popular music media (2009: 475). Rock music then enters into a form of heritage espoused most particularly by the collective cultural memory of baby-boomers, gathering further prominence and esteem in the eyes of their target market. At the same time, there is mounting evidence to suggest that the market for heritage rock is multi-generational, with younger fans consuming this style of popular music, often engaging with older listening formats and technologies, especially vinyl (see Bartmanski and Woodward 2015).

Jennings (2015) contends it is in fact the increase in the digital availability of music that drives dissolution of age divisions around music, "as musical signifiers lose their direct connection with time and space" (2015: 81). Through this lens, the lifetime soundtrack can be affected in two key ways through the stability of meaning and the regeneration of older rock music. The first is, as above, the reinforcement of musical taste and personal meaning which is achieved through the marketing of re-released music and associated acts and ephemera. The second is more integrated and relates back to the foundation of the lifetime soundtrack as pondered in Chapter 2: younger audiences of heritage rock may not have personal memories from the time of that music's original release; however, they may have mediated memories of their caregiver's experience, if this is how they first encountered it. Further to this though, teens and young adults are more than capable of finding heritage music on their own: many interviewees described listening to music that was before their time and forming their own memories, which are perhaps not as tied to progressions in music history, but rather to the cultural world in which they find themselves. Perfectly legitimate in their own right, these memories can still be evoked by the experience of the heritage touring act or album re-release, though they may forgo the tint of nostalgia that may be taken on in others' *older* memories. Hence, stability in the lifetime soundtrack for one generation, and the trickle-down effect of both memory and music marketing, has the potential to affect others in subtle and ongoing ways.

Conclusion

This chapter has discussed some of the most apparent ways in which the lifetime soundtrack in influenced by change and pays special attention to change that is evoked by ageing and the passage of time. The lifetime soundtrack develops through a process of canonization: this process can include temporarily pushing away those remembrances that no longer serve our current sense of self but can also include their re-integration if they regain personal meaning. Ageing can change the way we interact with and understand music, and it can also affect the way music is marketed to certain demographics. External factors that either restrict or facilitate music engagement, including music participation, can sometimes serve to reinforce parts of the lifetime soundtrack. Importantly, this can be emotionally variable. Though most of the interview extracts shown here portray a positivity towards music that is reinforced in the soundtrack, some people – like Ron – do not always find this dialogue helpful or necessary. The meaning of music and musical memories is vulnerable to the influence of ongoing life experiences. Whereas some people would like to predict that music will remain meaningful to them in the future, such as those who had chosen music for wedding or funeral ceremonies, there can be no certainty that this meaning will remain fixed. Contrastingly, the processes of canonization can affirm some cornerstones of the lifetime soundtrack, comprising music which maintains a steady, reciprocal relationship with a sense of self-identity. In these ways, the lifetime soundtrack is shown to be a flexible mnemonic connection, one that, despite continuous change, keeps its own record of life experiences, reflecting the growth of both body and mind of each individual.

7 Renewed Perspectives on Musical Memory

This book has endeavoured to trace the origins, processes and intricacies of a new framework for the study of music and autobiographical memory. The lifetime soundtrack is a fluid notion that not only helps to consolidate psychological and sociological theories that rationalize the strong connection between music and memory, but can also be used as a method for understanding multiple practices of reflexive meaning-making that occur alongside the consumption of music in everyday life. While previous research on autobiographical memory has been lacking in cultural sociology in favour of the concepts of cultural, collective or social memory, the interaction of music and memory in the field of psychology offers perspectives on how we might cognitively relate experience with musical sound. At the same time, scholarship in music sociology has made progress in the way of ethnographic insights on the production of self-identity through cultural collectives. The current research has drawn these fields together to produce a new understanding of how music integrates with the memory of individuals, in ways that have been shown to be both socially constructed yet uniquely meaningful on a personal level.

This research is concerned with the minutiae of the dialogue between music and memory, where it plays out in both routine tasks, and in peak experiences. The procedural side of this occurrence has been shown to be of dual mechanisms; on the one hand, musical memory can be environmentally triggered, where hearing music can bring back unanticipated thoughts and feelings about the past, with little control over the circumstances, or the response. These kinds of memories were discussed by participants as being instructive about both the power of music to play on their emotions, but also at the realization of how deeply music and memory were seeded in their minds. On the other hand, reflexive practices concerning musical memories occur as self-generated scenarios in which connecting music with experience is often more deliberate, though not necessarily enacted for a specific purpose. This happens, for example, when thinking about a relationship, person or place results in mindful reference to a song, album or artist that symbolizes an aspect thereof. More often though, a selection of recorded music for personal listening or sharing can reveal underlying memories that contribute to a person's overall feelings towards that music. The articulation of these processes throughout this book suggests that memory is often overlooked in the passages of everyday life, but moreover, that the opportunities presented by these events for personal meaning-making have not previously been well understood.

That participants expressed meaningful and complex feelings within interviews exemplifies the value of conducting in-depth qualitative research on this topic. Taking a different approach to van Dijck (2006) or Gabrielsson (2011), the research sought to explore participants' reactions in both the past and present, resembling the approach of Hays and Minichiello (2005) in their investigation of elderly persons' use of music. In undertaking my research interviews, it became apparent that emotionality within recollections is fluid, changing and developing over time. Some emotions fade, others are looked at anew, and still more can become intensified as they age. I contend that the passing of time acts upon emotionality in such a way that a deeper and more complex feeling or affect arises. To this end, I assert that the act of retrospection alters an individual's perception of experiences within memory, and the feelings that accompany it. In the process of remembering, emotionality that is experienced at the time of an event is filtered through the range of life experiences that have occurred since. Inherent in this is a practice of self-reflection, in which experiences and emotions are re-evaluated. The sensitivity that one may have to a memory and the affect that is subsequently perceived can be amplified or dampened through the acquisition of perspective. DeNora (2000) describes this process in a similar way; however, she emphasizes the direct engagement between music and the self, whereas I establish the intermediary juncture of memory as the agent responsible for the formulation of perspective. Additionally, the wider demographic of participants in my research expands upon DeNora's observation to illustrate that this process occurs in both men and women of various ages throughout adulthood.

To this end, the lifetime soundtrack has been defined here as a canonical collection of music and experience that helps us to frame past and current perspectives in methodical ways. Reflecting on the soundtrack helps to keep track of our personal challenges, triumphs, loves and sorrows, and continues to modulate, strengthen and evolve over the course of a life. Though there are few "hard and fast" guidelines for what is included or excluded, there are characteristics and themes that have been laid out throughout this book, and are here approximated into seven inter-related attributes.

Attributes of the Lifetime Soundtrack
Mediated foundations

The top-down mediation of music to children from caregivers in early life is the method through which the first additions to the lifetime soundtrack are typically made. The central location for music experience is often the home, and this is the site of much mediated music listening that forms the foundation of a personal soundtrack. Interviewees described a process of gradually stepping away from this pattern of music consumption as they gained the agency to choose music for themselves. The value placed upon music in the home should be considered as affecting the development of the lifetime soundtrack; despite the increased agency realized by most young people, the music preferences and reminiscing styles modelled by parents will inevitably have some influence on the lifetime soundtracks of young people in their care. Importantly though, the lifetime soundtrack is not determined solely by musical taste; certainly, music that is mediated to children is not guaranteed to become their preferred music, nor are the experiences that go along with it necessarily positive ones. From its inception, the lifetime soundtrack becomes a record that, despite ongoing processes of canonization, reminds us of associations that can provoke a range of feelings, particularly ones that are instructive, or aid expression and communication for ourselves and others.

Individual, yet socially constructed

The earliest memories of music and the related memory narrative are ultimately unlikely to be events that a person has any control over. It is from these beginnings that the lifetime soundtrack can be seen to sit, as van Dijck (2006) argues, at the intersection of both individual and collective cultural spheres. The difficulty in claiming music to be "autobiographical" in the age of global music distribution is that such a claim can be made by thousands of others – rendering your own experience perhaps a little less exclusive. Nonetheless, such connection with particular artists or music aids in the construction of subcultures and collectives, in which people can become sated with a feeling of belonging. The influence of collective musical memories is enacted not only within immediate family and friends, but also the media to which we are exposed at any stage of life that pushes an agenda regarding (especially commercialized) music. This is a space in which not just musical taste, but musical memory, can be capitalized upon. For baby-boomers in the early twenty-first century, the music market is redolent with the repackaging and continued promotion of rock music acts that reinforce the significance of lifetime soundtracks in both individuals and collectives, while promoting a nostalgic gaze amongst old and young fans alike. Despite the increasingly shared nature of lifetime soundtracks, the deeply personal understanding of what music means to each of us is something that cannot truly be duplicated in others. The complicated and ultra-specific circumstances in which we make and reflect on musical memories contribute not only to our sense of self, but to the continued feeling that our soundtrack could only ever describe the experiences of our own lifetime.

Emotion is dynamic and inherent

The connection between music, emotion and memory comprises a multitude of interactions that vary from person to person, dependent on factors such as personality, range of personal experiences and the importance of music to the individual. Emotion or affect was embedded in almost all memory narratives relayed by participants in this research; it is one factor that is so integrated into musical experience that it is difficult to discuss musical memories without referring to it. In this area, there is much that can be gleaned from music psychology; however, gaps in the explanation of all three elements – music, memory *and* emotion – remain. Just as the lifetime soundtrack can contain music outside of our personal taste, it is also imbued with a range of emotions associated with instances of happiness, grief, anger and so on. Contrary to the numerous studies that examine emotionality and memories, I found that the intensity of emotion varied in the narratives, such that high levels of emotion did not necessarily dictate the degree to which the scenario persisted in memory, though first experiences and important experiences were more easily recalled. Rather than acting as a catalyst, the lifetime soundtrack embodies emotion, rather than allowing music to act simply as a conduit for emotion. It is because of this embrace of affective musical memories that the lifetime soundtrack can be a compelling way of engaging with the meaning of personal experiences, especially in reflective practices later in life.

Linked to personal identity

As music sociologists have illustrated, music and listening practices are impacted and impact upon the development of personal identity. This has implications for the way we view the lifetime soundtrack, such that it can be understood as a continuum that may reflect the developing self over time. Articulated throughout the book is the idea that rehearsing or retelling memories in the present aids in the process of reassessing past attitudes and values, as stories morph and change with the ways in which we wish to be perceived by others. This is augmented when speaking about music, because music is so closely tied with personal explorations of who we are, or who we might want to be. Though a lot of this exploration occurs for many people during adolescence – when time is freed from greater adult responsibilities, the mind is open to suggestion, and attention can be focused on listening for hours at a time – there is continued opportunity to diversify music taste as time goes on. Certainly, there have been arguments to say that our music taste narrows with age, though other elements that might make it difficult to access and accept new music trends may also be at play.

The inter- and intra-personal role of musical memories was shown in memory narratives to encapsulate and express aspects of identity. This symbiotic relationship was most clearly evident when participants made projections about memories they planned to create in the future. Some individuals envisioned the use of music at a future occasion as representative of themselves or some aspect of their perceived identity with the goal of creating a memory imbued with specific affect that would be experienced by both themselves and others. Through in-depth engagement with this relationship on a micro-social level, my research demonstrates that memory and music work together in an interdependent relationship to aid identity development, and that the lifetime soundtrack is an effective way to explore and represent these processes.

Affected by modes of listening and responding to music

The lifetime soundtrack is not only affected by the kind of music we listen to, and who or what we associate it with, but our recollections of music are also influenced by the medium on which we most often listened to it. This can be explained to an extent by the cognitive workings of memory, where repeated experiences including sights, smells and sounds become the dominant memory over other experiences. Musical elements themselves can also be influential on how we remember music in the lifetime soundtrack, especially in recorded form. I contend that the contrast in authentic replication between memory and music is a significant factor leading to their integration. It is well documented in psychological literature that memories change over time; with each re-telling, details are added or dropped, exaggerated or neglected not only due to cognitive processing, but via the influence of collective remembering. In contrast, the internal elements of music itself which can act as an index for these memories remain static within various recorded forms.

Just as the methods through which we listen to music can help to memorialize both memory and emotion, so too can the ways we physically respond to music. Music that is part of our peak experiences can often provoke reactions such as crying, shivers or goose bumps; along with music, these sensations can further integrate events into memory. Other more purposeful movements – ones exemplified here by interviewees include dancing and military marching – have the added elements of pure embodiment and entrainment that assist in making and recalling memories. Music can come to represent an attitude or way of being through association of these things with a certain "sound", genre, artist or album, which over time becomes a solidified reference. Participants spoke of music that seemed to describe their situation at a certain time; this is evidenced not only in the narrative they weave, but also in the way that participants recognized, in the present tense, that specific songs or music represented broad yet distinct sectors of their life story. Instrumental elements too can denote aspects of experience in more covert ways. Sounds that aesthetically typify a certain genre or artist, for example distorted guitar riffs, can become referents for whole temporal periods that contain "collections" of autobiographical memory.

Musicianship and the value of music

Those who participate in music-making, either as their profession or as their hobby, may find that their interpretation of music and their mnemonic associations with it are affected by this experience. This occurs on a range of levels, including how music interfaces with their sense of identity, the recollection of music performance, or even the way they listen to music, armed with greater knowledge of music and recording technology. Musicians may embody both music and musical memories in corporeal ways, due to the involvement of the body in the production of most forms of music. This can influence how a musician creates and reflects upon their lifetime soundtrack. Further, I suggest that the value some individuals place on music plays a critical part in the quality of the lifetime soundtrack. In relation to my earlier point on cultural values imparted by caregivers in the home, it seems logical that the varying levels of engagement with music, and the perception of music as an adult, can impact on the depth and breadth of a lifetime soundtrack. For example, some participants held a strong opinion of their music tastes and maintained an enthusiasm for music that was part of the lifetime soundtrack and the memories that went with it. On the other hand, it seemed life experiences were less accessible through music for those who perceived music to have a low level of importance within their life, or who could be considered casual consumers. Both attitudes towards and engagement in music will impact the ways in which people consume music, which can in turn produce a variance in the way music integrates with memories, thereby altering an individual's relationship with their own soundtrack.

Maintained by reflexive memory practices

The lifetime soundtrack expands over time, while thoughts and feelings about its contents can sometimes morph and change as aspects of our sense of self alter in line with our environments and circumstances. In this way, the lifetime soundtrack is reflexive and fluid, rather than static, such that it is reflected on frequently in ways that help an individual make sense of their life experiences. At the same time, reflective practices shape the soundtrack through the process of canonization. This was revealed to be implicit within interviews, especially when participants were given the chance to evaluate the meaning of certain musical memories. Music allows us to revisit distinct moments in time where we can reflect on past ways of thinking and present ways of being. The integration of music into memory can also facilitate the encapsulation of entire eras of a life, or even a social trend, within a particular aesthetic tone. In this way, music aids the transcendence of temporal boundaries in memory, embodying atmospheres and affects that present opportunities for reflection and the development of personal perspective. The lifetime soundtrack offers an alternative way of reviewing a "life history", one that is at once more accessible and affectively nuanced than traditional forms such as written biographies. However, reflection on musical memory is often implicit, where music can reinforce mnemonic associations while being used as a catalyst for bonding, entertainment or emotional consolation. When the connection between autobiographical memory and music is perceived in this way, the extent to which both elements can aid in the construction of meaning for individuals becomes much greater than elucidated in previous research.

Gaps and opportunities: The future of the lifetime soundtrack

This research has laid out the concept of the lifetime soundtrack and applied it to the memory narratives of a moderately-sized group of participants in a Western context where mass-produced popular music was the prevailing genre in many people's musical experience. There are many more opportunities to apply the lifetime soundtrack to a range of contexts where music and memory intersect, through which we may find further ways to consolidate the concept of the lifetime soundtrack. Certainly, in the context of the modernization of music production, distribution and consumption where change is occurring with increasing speed, it will be necessary to re-evaluate the process of lifetime soundtrack creation as well as characteristics of reflexive practices for the next generation. Similarly, more recent trends in music-making, including the increasingly globalized DIY movement, advances in production technologies, and the growing instability of cultural economies (Mōri 2009; Strachan 2007) may affect not just the production of music but the way in which those who make music reflect upon their practices through their lifetime soundtrack.

There is also a need to consider how the lifetime soundtracks may be enacted for people in non-Western cultures. At the start of the book I acknowledged that research participants were predominantly of Anglo-European backgrounds, and few people spoke of music outside of Western traditions. The application of the lifetime soundtrack within other cultures presents an opportunity to explore not only the ways in which music may be perceived, memorialized and even function in different ways (see Boer and Fischer 2012), but also how cultures of remembering may interact in a range of ways with music. For example, Wang and Conway (2004) reveal the contrasts between Chinese and American autobiographical stories, where Chinese stories were less individually focused, speaking more of social or historical moments, and more morally directive than American narratives. It would be worth considering too how the lifetime soundtrack itself may manifest in different ways within cultures outside the West. For instance, how might traditions like the Carnatic music of India, whose structures, elements and applications are vastly different from those found in Western music, interact with personal affects and life events? How might performers of this music remember their performance, particularly when they are paid? And how might traditional and popular musics be present in the home and other spaces of everyday life for people living in other parts of the world? Spiritual or religious musics, particularly of non-Western cultures, may interact in distinct ways with autobiographical, as well as collective memory (see, for example, Waugh 2005) and would therefore act as a rich area in which to apply the lifetime soundtrack framework. Clearly, there is the potential for the lifetime soundtrack to be enacted outside the boundaries of its original creation such that it could provide great insights into the formation of, and reflection upon, musical autobiographical memories.

Besides looking to the emergence of the lifetime soundtrack in other cultures, another relevant and practical application of music and memory theories raised in this research comes in the form of well-being and aged care. For example, the use of musical memories as reflexive tools for meaning-making can be drawn upon for therapeutic purposes to influence things like mood, a sense of personal identity, and a sense of agency. Currently, music is used to various effect within health care settings to help manage emotional and behavioural issues such as agitation, anxiety and depression in elderly people (e.g. Cooke *et al.* 2010; Cohen-Mansfield *et al.* 2015; Rawtaer *et al.* 2015). Many studies have established the positive effects of music upon autobiographical recall and elements of well-being in those with dementia (e.g. El Haj, Fasotti and Allain 2012; García *et al.* 2011; Groarke and Hogan 2015; Shibazaki and Marshall 2017), though the majority of scholarship lacks a theoretical rationale or inclusion of qualitative assessment of resulting well-being outcomes (Istvandity 2017b). With group-based therapies dominating trials and real-life applications, there has been a move towards individual-based therapy programmes to facilitate a greater emphasis on personalized care (Sakamoto *et al.* 2013; Hsu *et al.* 2015).

The current research provides qualitative evidence of the connection between memory and music that could be used to supplement music therapy and music reminiscence programmes. Most significantly, this research underscores that the use of music to reflect on memories promotes a sense of agency within an individual, and a sense of belonging within a society. This research also has the potential to unlock new avenues through which to consider the range of ways individuals interact with music from sociological perspectives. In particular, there is much work to be done connecting individual and collective experience in cultural activity, where memory is often overlooked as a significant catalyst in processes of identity development, emotional response and music-making. The interdisciplinary approach adopted by this research is evidence of the new knowledge waiting to be conceptualized and articulated through the careful positioning of music, memory and identity at the intersection of the personal and the collective, between social and psychological. To this end, it also contributes new avenues of inquiry to memory studies, which, while supportive of interdisciplinary scholarship of music, still has further capacity to embrace more fully the opportunities presented by memory and music through the range of social, psychological, historical and ethnographic lenses available.

Conclusion

This book has explored the deeply biographical and affective narratives that connect with music in a range of contexts, offered up by young and older adults who all felt the similar impact of music not only upon their life, but upon their memories. Their stories depict a reliance on music in daily life, in troubling times and in celebration, which suggests the value of music for making sense of our lives is incredibly high, yet somewhat under-recognized. In a time of increasing availability of music, there has been a surge in the ability to use soundtracks more reflexively than ever, though it is hoped that this can be sustained as a way of enriching lives, rather than diluting our musical experiences. The lifetime soundtrack is presented here as a new addition to scholarship in the area of music and memory studies. By drawing on sociological and psychological theories of memory, music and emotion, this research produces an interdisciplinary understanding of musical memories, which have been shown not only to aid the construction of identity but also to inform perspective on autobiographical experience and facilitate personal interpretation of the life story. Though the coupling of music and memory has long been referred to anecdotally, and mentioned briefly within other scholarship, its conceptualization as the framework of the lifetime soundtrack provides a useful tool for the continued examination of musical memories in everyday life.

Bibliography

Adamson, Sue, and Margaret Holloway. 2012. "'A Sound Track of your Life': Music in Contemporary UK Funerals". *Omega* 35/1: 33–54.

Alea, Nicole, and Susan Bluck. 2003. "Why are you Telling me That? A Conceptual Model of the Social Function of Autobiographical Memory". *Memory* 11/2: 165–78.

Almond, Brenda. 2006. *The Fragmenting Family*. Oxford: Oxford University Press.

Anderson, Ben. 2004. "Recorded Music and Practices of Remembering". *Social and Cultural Geography* 5/1: 3–20.

Arrow, Michelle. 2005. "'Everything Stopped for *Blue Hills*': Radio, Memory and Australian Women's Domestic Lives, 1944–2001". *Australian Feminist Studies* 20/48: 305–318.

Ashforth, Blake E., and Ronald H. Humphrey. 1993. "Emotional Labor in Service Roles: The Influence of Identity". *Academy of Management Review* 18/1: 88–115.

Assmann, Aleida. 2006. "Memory, Individual and Collective". In *The Oxford Handbook of Contextual Political Analysis*, edited by Robert E. Goodin and Charles Tilly, 210–26. Oxford: Oxford University Press.

Atkinson, Robert. 1998. *The Life Story Interview*. Sage University Papers Series on Qualitative Research Methods, 44. Thousand Oaks, CA: Sage.

Baker, Sarah Louise. 2004. "Pop in(to) the Bedroom: Popular Music in Pre-teen Girls' Bedroom Culture". *European Journal of Cultural Studies* 7/1: 75–93.

Bala, Nicholas, and Rebecca Jaremko Bromwich. 2002. "Context and Inclusivity in Canada's Evolving Definition of the Family". *International Journal of Law, Policy and the Family* 16: 145–80.

Baraldi, Filippo Bonini. 2009. "All the Pain and Joy of the World in a Single Melody: A Transylvanian Case Study on Musical Emotion". *Music Perception* 26/3: 257–61.

Barbalet, Jack. 2005. "Weeping and Transformations of the Self". *Journal for the Theory of Social Behaviour* 35/2: 125–41.

Barni, Daniela, Sonia Ranieri, Eugenia Scabini and Rosa Rosnati. 2011. "Value Transmission in the Family: Do Adolescents Accept the Values their Parents Want to Transmit". *Journal of Moral Education* 40/1: 105–121.

Barrett, Margaret S. 2009. "Sounding Lives in and Through Music: A Narrative Inquiry of the 'Everyday' Musical Engagement of a Young Child". *Journal of Early Childhood Research* 7/2: 115–34.

Barrett, F. S., K. J. Grimm, R. W. Robins, T. Wildschut, C. Sedikides and P. Janata. 2010. "Music-evoked Nostalgia: Affect, Memory, and Personality". *Emotion* 10/3: 390–403.

Bartmanski, Dominik, and Ian Woodward. 2015. "The Vinyl: The Analogue Medium in the Age of Digital Reproduction". *Journal of Consumer Culture* 15/1: 3–27.

Barton, Rebecca. 2004. "The Aging Musician". *Work* 22: 131–38.

Baumgartner, Hans. 1992. "Remembrance of Things Past: Music, Autobiographical Memory, and Emotion". *Advances in Consumer Research* 19/1: 613–20.

Bayton, Mavis. 1997. "Women and the Electric Guitar". In *Sexing the Groove: Popular Music and Gender,* edited by Sheila Whiteley, 37–49. London and New York: Routledge.

Becker, Howard S. 1951. "The Professional Dance Musician and his Audience". *American Journal of Sociology* 57/2: 136–44.

Belfi, Amy M., Brett Karlan and Daniel Tranel. 2016. "Music Evokes Vivid Autobiographical Memories". *Memory* 24/7: 979–89.

Bennett, Andy. 2000. *Popular Music and Youth Culture: Music, Identity and Place.* London: Macmillan.

—2008. "'Things they do look awful cool': Ageing Rock Icons and Contemporary Youth Audiences". *Leisure/Loisir* 32/2: 259–78.

—2009. "'Heritage Rock': Rock Music, Representation and Heritage Discourse". *Poetics* 37/5-6: 474–89.

—2013. *Music, Style, and Aging: Growing Old Disgracefully?* Philadelphia: Temple University Press.

Bennett, Andy, and Paul Hodkinson, eds. 2012. *Ageing and Youth Cultures: Music, Style and Identity.* London and New York: Berg.

Bennett, Andy, and Ian Rogers. 2016. "Popular Music and Materiality: Memorabilia and Memory Traces". *Popular Music and Society* 39/1: 28–42.

Berntsen, Dorthe. 1996. "Involuntary Autobiographical Memories". *Applied Cognitive Psychology* 10: 435–54.

Bloom, Arvid J., and Paula Skutnick-Henley. 2005. "Facilitating Flow Experiences among Musicians". *American Music Teacher* 54/5: 24–28.

Bluck, Susan. 2003. "Autobiographical Memory: Exploring its Functions in Everyday Life". *Memory* 11/2: 113–23.

Bluck, Susan, and Tilmann Habermas. 2001. "Extending the Study of Autobiographical Memory: Thinking Back about Life across the Life Span". *Review of General Psychology* 5/2: 135–47.

Boer, Diana, and Ronald Fischer. 2012. "Towards a Holistic Model of Functions of Music Listening across Cultures: A Culturally Decentred Qualitative Approach". *Psychology of Music* 40/2: 179–200.

Boer, Diana, Ronald Fischer, Micha Strack, Michael H. Bond, Eva Lo and Jason Lam. 2011. "How Shared Preferences in Music Create Bonds between People: Values as the Missing Link". *Personality and Social Psychology Bulletin* 37/9: 1159–171.

Bourdieu, Pierre. 1984. *Distinction: A Social Critique of the Judgement of Taste.* London: Routledge.

Bowlby, Sophie, Susan Gregory and Linda McKie. 1997. "'Doing Home': Patriarchy, Caring, and Space". *Women's Studies International Forum* 20/3: 343–50.

Brockmeier, Jens. 2010. "After the Archive: Remapping Memory". *Culture & Psychology* 16/1: 5–35.

Brown, Roger, and James Kulik. 1977. "Flashbulb Memories". *Cognition* 5/1: 73–99.

Bull, Michael. 2004. "Automobility and the Power of Sound". *Theory, Culture & Society* 21/4-5: 243–59.

—2007. *Sound Moves: iPod Culture and Urban Experience.* London and New York: Routledge.

—2009. "The Auditory Nostalgia of iPod Culture". In *Sound Souvenirs: Audio Technologies, Memory and Cultural Practices,* edited by Karin Bijsterveld and José van Dijck, 83–93. Amsterdam: Amsterdam University Press.

Cady, Elizabeth T., Richard Jackson Harris and J. Bret Knappenberger. 2008. "Using Music to Cue Autobiographical Memories of Different Lifetime Periods". *Psychology of Music* 36/2: 157–77.

Caswell, Glenys. 2012. "Beyond Words: Some Uses of Music in the Funeral Setting". *OMEGA-Journal of Death and Dying* 64/4: 319–34.

Clayton, Martin, Rebecca Sager and Udo Will. 2005. "In Time with the Music: The Concept of Entrainment and its Significance for Ethnomusicology". *European Meetings in Ethnomusicology* 11/1: 1–82.

Clift, Stephen, and Grenville Hancox. 2010. "The Significance of Choral Singing for Sustaining Psychological Wellbeing: Findings from a Survey of Choristers in England, Australia and Germany". *Music Performance Research* 3/1: 79–96.

Cohen, Gillian. 1996. *Memory in the Real World*. East Sussex: Psychology Press.

Cohen, Sara. 1991. *Rock Culture in Liverpool: Popular Music in the Making*. Oxford: Clarendon Press.

—1997. "Men Making a Scene: Rock Music and the Production of Gender". In *Sexing the Groove: Popular Music and Gender*, edited by Sheila Whiteley, 17–36. London and New York: Routledge.

Cohen-Mansfield, Jiska, Marcia S. Marx, Maha Dakheel-Ali and Khin Thein. 2015. "The Use and Utility of Specific Nonpharmacological Interventions for Behavioral Symptoms in Dementia: An Exploratory Study". *American Journal of Geriatric Psychiatry* 23/2: 160–70.

Connell, Matt. 2012. "Talking about Old Records: Generational Musical Identity among Older People". *Popular Music* 31/2: 261–78.

Conway, Martin A. 1990. *Autobiographical Memory*. Milton Keynes: Open University Press.

—2009. "Episodic Memories". *Neuropsychologia* 47/11: 2305–313.

Cook, Nicholas. 1998. *Music: A Very Short Introduction*. Oxford: Oxford University Press.

Cooke, Marie L., Wendy Moyle, David H. K. Shum, Scott D. Harrison and Jenny E. Murfield. 2010. "A Randomized Controlled Trial Exploring the Effect of Music on Agitated Behaviours and Anxiety in Older People with Dementia". *Aging and Mental Health* 14/8: 905–916.

Cotter, Katherine N., Paul J. Silvia and Kirill Fayn. 2018a. "What Does Feeling Like Crying When Listening to Music Feel Like?" *Psychology of Aesthetics, Creativity, and the Arts* 12/2: 216–27.

Cotter, Katherine N., Alyssa N. Prince, Alexander P. Christensen and Paul J. Silvia. 2018b. "Feeling Like Crying When Listening to Music: Exploring Musical and Contextual Features". *Empirical Studies of the Arts*. https://doi.org/10.1177%2F0276237418805692

Coutinho, Eduardo, and Klaus R. Scherer. 2017. "The Effect of Context and Audio-visual Modality on Emotions Elicited by a Musical Performance". *Psychology of Music* 45/4: 550–69.

Csikszentmihalyi, Mihaly. 1997. "Happiness and Creativity: Going with the Flow". *The Futurist* 31/5: 8–12.

—2000. "Flow". In *Encyclopedia of Psychology*, vol. 3. Washington: American Psychological Association.

Cuddy, Lola L., and Jacalyn Duffin. 2005. "Music, Memory, and Alzheimer's Disease: Is

Music Recognition Spared in Dementia, and How Can it be Assessed?" *Medical Hypotheses* 64/2: 229–35.

Cutas, Daniela, and Sarah Chan. 2012. "Introduction: Perspectives on Private and Family Life". In *Families: Beyond the Nuclear Ideal*, edited by Daniela Cutas and Sarah Chan, 1–12. Huntington: Bloomsbury Academic.

Damousi, Joy, and Paula Hamilton, eds. 2017. *A Cultural History of Sound, Memory, and the Senses*. London and New York: Routledge.

Davidson, Jane W. 2005. "Bodily Communication in Musical Performance". In *Musical Communication*, edited by Dorothy Miell, Raymond MacDonald and David J. Hargreaves, 215–37. Oxford: Oxford University Press.

DeCasper, Anthony J., Jean-Pierre Lecanuet, Marie-Claire Busnel, Carolyn Granier-Deferre and Roselyne Maugeais. 1994. "Fetal Reactions to Recurrent Maternal Speech". *Infant Behavior and Development* 17/2: 159–64.

DeChaine, D. Robert. 2002. "Affect and Embodied Understanding in Musical Experience". *Text and Performance Quarterly* 22/2: 79–98.

DeNora, Tia. 2000. *Music in Everyday Life*. Cambridge: Cambridge University Press.

DiMaggio, Paul, and Michael Useem. 1978. "Social Class and Arts Consumption". *Theory and Society* 5/2: 141–61.

Drummond, John D. 1990. "The Characteristics of Amateur and Professional". *International Journal of Music Education* 15/1: 3–8.

El Haj, Mohamad, Pascal Antoine, Jean Louis Nandrino, Marie-Christine Gély-Nargeot and Stéphane Raffard. 2015. "Self-defining Memories during Exposure to Music in Alzheimer's Disease". *International Psychogeriatrics* 27/10: 1719–730.

El Haj, Mohamad, Luciano Fasotti and Philippe Allain. 2012. "The Involuntary Nature of Music-evoked Autobiographical Memories in Alzheimer's Disease". *Consciousness and Cognition* 21/1: 238–46.

Elliott, Diana M. 1997. "Traumatic Events: Prevalence and Delayed Recall in the General Population". *Journal of Consulting and Clinical Psychology* 65/5: 811–20.

Emke, Ivan. 2002. "Why the Sad Face? Secularization and the Changing Function of Funerals in Newfoundland". *Mortality: Promoting the Interdisciplinary Study of Death and Dying* 7/3: 269–84.

Emmerich, Edeltraut, Lars Rudel and Frank Richter. 2008. "Is the Audiologic Status of Professional Musicians a Reflection of the Noise Exposure in Classical Orchestral Music?" *European Archives of Oto-Rhino-Laryngology* 265/7: 753–58.

Emmers, Tara M., and Russell D. Hart. 1996. "Romantic Relationship Disengagement and Coping Rituals". *Communication Research Reports* 13/1: 8–18.

Erikson, Erik Homburger. 1959. *Identity and the Life Cycle: Selected Papers*. Oxford: International Universities Press.

Eroglu, Sevgin A., Karen A. Machleit and Jean-Charles Chebat. 2005. "The Interaction of Retail Density and Music Tempo: Effects on Shopper Responses". *Psychology & Marketing* 22/7: 577–89.

Faulkner, Robert R., and Howard S. Becker. 2009. *"Do You Know...?" The Jazz Repertoire in Action*. Chicago and London: The University of Chicago Press.

Featherstone, Mike. 2006. "Archive". *Theory, Culture & Society* 23/2-3: 591–96.

Finnegan, Ruth. 2007. *The Hidden Musicians: Music-making in an English Town*. Middletown, CT: Wesleyan University Press.

Fivush, Robyn. 2008. "Remembering and Reminiscing: How Individual Lives are Constructed in Family Narratives". *Memory Studies* 1/1: 49–58.

—2011. "The Development of Autobiographical Memory". *Annual Review of Psychology* 62: 559–82.

Forman, Murray. 2012. "'How We Feel the Music': Popular Music by Elders and for Elders". *Popular Music* 31/2: 245–60.

Frith, Simon. 1981. *Sound Effects: Youth, Leisure, and the Politics of Rock'n'roll*. New York: Pantheon Books.

—1986. "Why Do Songs Have Words". *Contemporary Music Review* 5/1: 77–96.

—1987. "Towards an Aesthetic of Popular Music". In *Music and Society: The Politics of Composition, Performance and Reception*, edited by Richard Leppert and Susan McClary, 133–49. Cambridge: Cambridge University Press.

—1996. "Music and Identity". In *Questions of Cultural Identity*, edited by S. Hall and P. du Gay, 108–128. London: Sage Publications.

—1998. *Performing Rites: On the Value of Popular Music*. Cambridge: Harvard University Press.

—2002. "Music and Everyday Life". *Critical Quarterly* 44/1: 35–48.

Gabrielsson, A. 2011. *Strong Experiences with Music: Music is Much More than Just Music*, translated by Rod Bradbury. Oxford: Oxford University Press.

García, Juan José Meilán, Rosario Iodice, Juan Carro, José Antonio Sánchez, Francisco Palmero and Ana María Mateos. 2011. "Improvement of Autobiographic Memory Recovery by Means of Sad Music in Alzheimer's Disease Type Dementia". *Aging Clinical and Experimental Research* 24/3: 227–32.

Garrido, Sandra, and Jane W. Davidson. 2016. "The Modern Funeral and Music for Celebration". In *Music and Mourning*, edited by Jane W. Davidson and Sandra Garrido, 9–17. London and New York: Routledge.

Gates, J. Terry. 1991. "Music Participation: Theory, Research, and Policy". *Bulletin of the Council for Research in Music Education* 109: 1–35.

Gembris, Heiner. 2008. "Musical Activities in the Third Age: An Empirical Study with Amateur Musicians". *Second European Conference on Developmental Psychology of Music*. London: University of Roehampton.

Giddens, Anthony. 1991. *Modernity and Self-identity: Self and Society in the Late Modern Age*. Stanford, CA: Stanford University Press.

Groarke, Jenny M., and Michael J. Hogan. 2015. "Enhancing Wellbeing: An Emerging Model of the Adaptive Functions of Music Listening". *Psychology of Music* 44/4: 769–91.

Groves, Robert M., Floyd J. Fowler Jr, Mick P. Couper, James M. Lepkowski, Eleanor Singer and Roger Tourangeau. 2004. *Survey Methodology*. New Jersey: John Wiley & Sons.

Gvion, Liora. 2016. "'If you ever saw an Opera singer naked': The Social Construction of the Singer's Body". *European Journal of Cultural Studies* 19/2: 150–69.

Habermas, Tilmann, and Susan Bluck. 2000. "Getting a Life: The Emergence of the Life Story in Adolescence". *Psychological Bulletin* 126/5: 748–69.

Halbwachs, Maurice. 1992. *On Collective Memory*, translated by Lewis A. Coser. Chicago and London: The University of Chicago Press.

Hallam, Susan. 2010. "The Power of Music: Its Impact on the Intellectual, Social and Personal Development of Children and Young People". *International Journal of Music Education* 28/3: 269–89.

Hargreaves, David J., and Adrian C. North. 1999. "The Functions of Music in Everyday Life: Redefining the Social in Music Psychology". *Psychology of Music* 27/1: 71–83.

Harrison, Jill, and John Ryan. 2010. "Musical Taste and Ageing". *Ageing & Society* 30/4: 649–69.

Hays, Terrence, and Victor Minichiello. 2005. "The Meaning of Music in the Lives of Older People: A Qualitative Study". *Psychology of Music* 33/4: 437–51.

Hesmondhalgh, David. 2008. "Towards a Critical Understanding of Music, Emotion and Self-identity". *Consumption, Markets and Culture* 11/4: 329–43.

—2013. *Why Music Matters*. West Sussex: John Wiley & Sons.

Hesmondhalgh, David, and Sarah Baker. 2010. "'A Very Complicated Version of Freedom': Conditions and Experiences of Creative Labour in Three Cultural Industries". *Poetics* 38/1: 4–20.

—2011. *Creative Labour: Media Work in Three Cultural Industries*. London and New York: Routledge.

Hochschild, Arlie Russell. 2003. *The Managed Heart: Commercialization of Human Feeling*. California and London: University of California Press [1983].

Hogarty, Jean. 2016. *Popular Music and Retro Culture in the Digital Era*. London: Routledge.

Hoge, Dean R., Gregory H. Petrillo and Ella I. Smith. 1982. "Transmission of Religious and Social Values from Parents to Teenage Children". *Journal of Marriage and Family* 44/3: 569–80.

Holloway, Margaret, Susan Adamson, Vassos Argyrou, Peter Draper and Daniel Mariau. 2013. "'Funerals aren't nice but it couldn't have been nicer': The Makings of a Good Funeral". *Mortality: Promoting the Interdisciplinary Study of Death and Dying* 18/1: 30–53.

Homan, Shane. 2006. *Access All Eras: Tribute Bands and Global Pop Culture: Tribute Bands and Global Pop Culture*. New York: McGraw-Hill Education.

Hornby, Nick. 1995. *High Fidelity*. London: Victor Gollancz.

Horton, Donald. 1990. "The Dialogue of Courtship in Popular Song". In *On Record: Rock, Pop and the Written Word*, edited by Simon Frith and Andrew Goodwin, 11–21. London and New York: Routledge [1957].

Howarth, Glennys. 2000. "Dismantling the Boundaries between Life and Death". *Morality* 5/2: 127–38.

Hudson, Ray. 2006. "Regions and Place: Music, Identity and Place". *Progress in Human Geography* 30/5: 626–34.

Hsu, Ming Hung, Rosamund Flowerdew, Michael Parker, Jörg Fachner and Helen Odell-Miller. 2015. "Individual Music Therapy for Managing Neuropsychiatric Symptoms for People with Dementia and their Carers: A Cluster Randomised Controlled Feasibility Study". *BMC Geriatrics* 15/1: 84–103.

Huron, David. 2001. "Is Music an Evolutionary Adaptation?" *Annals of the New York Academy of Sciences* 930/1: 43–61.

—2006. *Sweet Anticipation: Music and the Psychology of Expectation*. Cambridge: MIT Press.

Istvandity, Lauren. 2014. "The Lifetime Soundtrack: Music as an Archive for Autobiographical Memory". *Popular Music History* 9/2: 136–54.

—2017a. "Musicians and the Lifetime Soundtrack: Creation and Perception of Musically Motivated Autobiographical Memories". *Perfect Beat* 18/1: 49–68.

—2017b. "Combining Music and Reminiscence Therapy Interventions for Wellbeing in Elderly Populations: A Systematic Review". *Complementary Therapies in Clinical Practice* 28: 18–25.

—2019. "The Lifetime Soundtrack 'on the Move': Music, Autobiographical Memory and Mobilities". *Memory Studies* 15/1.

Janata, Petr. 2009. "The Neural Architecture of Music-evoked Autobiographical Memories". *Cerebral Cortex* 19/11: 2579–594.

Janata, Petr, Stefan T. Tomic and Sonja K. Rakowski. 2007. "Characterisation of Music-evoked Autobiographical Memories". *Memory* 15/8: 845–60.

Jennings, Ros. 2015. "Popular Music and Ageing". In *The Routledge Handbook of Cultural Gerontology*, edited by Julia Twigg and Wendy Martin, 77–84. New York and London: Routledge.

Jennings, Ros, and Abigail Gardner, eds. 2012. *'Rock On': Women, Ageing and Popular Music*. New York and London: Routledge.

Jorgensen, Estelle R. 1993. "On Building Social Theories of Music Education". *Bulletin of the Council for Research in Music Education* 116 (Spring): 33–50.

Juniu, Susana, Ted Tedrick and Rosangela Boyd. 1996. "Leisure or Work? Amateur and Professional Musicians' Perception of Rehearsal and Performance". *Journal of Leisure Research* 28/1: 44–56.

Juslin, Patrik N., and John Sloboda, eds. 2010. *Handbook of Music and Emotion: Theory, Research, Applications*. Oxford: Oxford University Press.

Kalish, Richard A., and Ann I. Johnson. 1972. "Value Similarities and Differences in Three Generations of Women". *Journal of Marriage and Family* 34/1: 49–54.

Kärjä, Antti-Ville. 2006. "A Prescribed Alternative Mainstream: Popular Music and Canon Formation". *Popular Music* 25/1: 3–19.

Kassabian, Anahid. 2013. *Ubiquitous Listening: Affect, Attention, and Distributed Listening*. Berkeley, Los Angeles and London: University of California Press.

Keightley, Emily, and Michael Pickering. 2006. "For the Record: Popular Music and Photography as Technologies of Memory". *European Journal of Cultural Studies* 9/2: 149–65.

—2012. *The Mnemonic Imagination: Remembering as Creative Practice*. Basingstoke: Palgrave Macmillan.

Kelley, Jonathan, and Ian McAllister. 1985. "Class and Party in Australia: Comparison with Britain and the USA". *British Journal of Sociology* 36/3: 383–420.

Knobloch, Silvia, and Dolf Zillmann. 2003. "Appeal of Love Themes in Popular Music". *Psychological Reports* 93/3: 653–58.

Koivunen, Niina, and Grete Wennes. 2011. "Show us the Sound! Aesthetic Leadership of Symphony Orchestra Conductors". *Leadership* 7/1: 51–71.

Krumhansl, Carol Lynne, and Justin Adam Zupnick. 2013. "Cascading Reminiscence Bumps in Popular Music". *Psychological Science* 24/10: 2057–68.

Kusumi, Takashi, Ken Matsuda and Eriko Sugimori. 2010. "The Effects of Aging on Nostalgia in Consumers' Advertisement Processing". *Japanese Psychological Research* 52/3: 150–62.

Laland, Kevin, Clive Wilkins and Nicky Clayton. 2016. "The Evolution of Dance". *Current Biology* 26/1: R5–R9.

Lipe, Hillary. P. 1980. "The Function of Weeping in the Adult". *Nursing Forum* 19/1: 26–44.

Loftus, Elizabeth F. 1975. "Leading Questions and the Eyewitness Report". *Cognitive Psychology* 7/4: 560–72.

—1993. "The Reality of Repressed Memories". *American Psychologist* 48/5: 518–37.

—2005. "Planting Misinformation in the Human Mind: A 30-Year Investigation of the Malleability of Memory". *Learning and Memory* 12: 361–66.

McAdams, Dan. P. 2001. "The Psychology of Life Stories". *Review of General Psychology* 5/2: 100–122.

—2005. "Studying Lives in Time: A Narrative Approach". In *Advances in Life Course Research*, edited by Rene Levy, Paolo Ghisletta, Jean-Marie Le Goff, Dario Spini and Eric Widmer, 237–58. Oxford: Elsevier Ltd.

—2008. "Personal Narratives and the Life Story". In *Handbook of Personality: Theory and Research*, edited by O. P. John, R. W. Robins and L. A. Pervin, 242–62. New York: Guilford Press.

McDermott, Orii, Nadia Crellin, Hanne Mette Ridder and Martin Orrell. 2013. "Music Therapy in Dementia: A Narrative Synthesis Systematic Review". *International Journal of Geriatric Psychiatry* 28/8: 781–94.

McMillan, Paul Andrew. 2015. "Why Cover? An Ethnographic Exploration of Identity Politics Surrounding 'Covers' and 'Originals' Music in Dunedin, New Zealand". *MEDIANZ: Media Studies Journal of Aotearoa New Zealand* 15/1: 35–53.

McRobbie, Angela, and Jenny Garber. 1976. "Girls and Subcultures". In *Resistance through Rituals: Youth Subcultures in Post-war Britain*, edited by Stuart Hall and Tony Jefferson, 209–222. London: Hutchinson.

Madsen, Clifford K., Suzanne R. Byrnes, Deborah A. Capperella-Sheldon and Ruth V. Brittin. 1993. "Aesthetic Response to Music: Musicians versus Nonmusicians". *Journal of Music Therapy* 30/3: 174–91.

Mallett, Shelley. 2004. "Understanding Home: A Critical Review of the Literature". *The Sociological Review* 52/1: 62–89.

Maslen, Sarah. 2013. "'Playing Like a Girl': Practices and Performance Ideals at the Piano". *Performance Enhancement & Health* 2/1: 3–7.

Merriam, Alan P. 1964. *The Anthropology of Music*. Evanston, IL: Northwestern University Press.

Merriam Webster Dictionary. 2018. "Nostalgia". https://www.merriam-webster.com/dictionary/nostalgia

Michels-Ratliff, Emelia, and Michael Ennis. 2016. "This is Your Song: Using Participants' Music Selections to Evoke Nostalgia and Autobiographical Memories Efficiently". *Psychomusicology: Music, Mind, and Brain* 26/4: 379–84.

Misztal, Barbara A. 2003. *Theories of Social Remembering*. Maidenhead; Philadelphia: Open University Press.

Mithen, Steven. 2006. *The Singing Neanderthals: The Origin of Music, Language, Mind and Body*. London: Phoenix Books.

Mohr, John, and Paul DiMaggio. 1995. "The Intergenerational Transmission of Cultural Capital". *Research in Social Stratification and Mobility* 14: 167–200.

Morgan, Jill P., Raymond A. R. MacDonald and Stephanie E. Pitts. 2015. "'Caught between a Scream and a Hug': Women's Perspectives on Music Listening and Interaction with Teenagers in the Family Unit". *Psychology of Music* 43/5: 611–26.

Mōri, Yoshitaka. 2009. "J-pop: From the Ideology of Creativity to DiY Music Culture". *Inter-Asia Cultural Studies* 10/4: 474–88.

Nagel, Ineke, and Harry B. G. Ganzeboom. 2002. "Participation in Legitimate Culture: Family and School Effects from Adolescence to Adulthood". *The Netherlands' Journal of Social Sciences* 38/2: 102–120.

Nelson, Katherine. 1993. "The Psychological and Social Origins of Autobiographical Memory". *Psychological Science* 4/1: 7–14.

Nelson, Katherine, and Robyn Fivush. 2004. "The Emergence of Autobiographical Memory: A Social Cultural Developmental Theory". *Psychological Review* 111/2: 486–511.

Nijs, Luc, Micheline Lesaffre and Marc Leman. 2009. *The Musical Instrument as a Natural Extension of the Musician*. The 5th Conference of Interdisciplinary Musicology, LAM-Institut Jean Le Rond d'Alembert.

Nora, Pierre. 1989. "Between Memory and History: Les Lieux de Memoire". *Representations* 26/Spring: 7–24.

North, Adrian. C., and David J. Hargreaves. 1999. "Music and Adolescent Identity". *Music Education Research* 1/1: 75–92.

Nusbaum, Emily C., Paul J. Silvia, Roger E. Beaty, Chris J. Burgin, Donald A. Hodges and Thomas R. Kwapil. 2014. "Listening between the Notes: Aesthetic Chills in Everyday Music Listening". *Psychology of Aesthetics, Creativity, and the Arts* 8/1: 104.

O'Callaghan, Clare C., Fiona McDermott, Peter Hudson and John R. Zalcberg. 2013. "Sound Continuing Bonds with the Deceased: The Relevance of Music, Including Preloss Music Therapy, for Eight Bereaved Caregivers". *Death Studies* 37/2: 101–125.

Palin, S. L. 1994. "Does Classical Music Damage the Hearing of Musicians? A Review of the Literature". *Occupational Medicine* 44/3: 130–36.

Parkes, Colin Murray, and Holly G. Prigerson. 2013. *Bereavement: Studies of Grief in Adult Life*. London and New York: Routledge.

Parsons, B. 2008. "Music at Funerals: The Challenge of Keeping in Tune with the Needs of the Bereaved". In *Death Our Future: Christian Theology and Funeral Practice*, edited by Peter C. Jupp, 202–211. London: Epworth.

Peterson, Richard A., and Roger M. Kern. 1996. "Changing Highbrow Taste: From Snob to Omnivore". *American Sociological Review* 61/5: 900–907.

Phillips-Silver, Jessica, C. Athena Aktipis and Gregory A. Bryant. 2010. "The Ecology of Entrainment: Foundations of Coordinated Rhythmic Movement". *Music Perception* 28/1: 3–14.

Pickering, Michael, and Emily Keightley. 2006. "The Modalities of Nostalgia". *Current Sociology* 54/6: 919–41.

—2015. *Photography, Music and Memory: Pieces of the Past in Everyday Life*. Basingstoke: Palgrave Macmillan.

Pillemer, David B. 1998. *Momentous Events, Vivid Memories*. Cambridge, MA and London: Harvard University Press.

—2001. "Momentous Events and the Life Story". *Review of General Psychology* 5/2: 123–34.

Pitts, Stephanie. 2016. "Starting a Music Degree at University". In *The Music Practitioner: Research for the Music Performer, Teacher and Listener*, edited by Jane W. Davidson, 215–24. London and New York: Routledge.

Quinlan, Michael. 2016. "Marriage, Tradition, Multiculturalism and the Accommodation of Difference in Australia". *University of Notre Dame Australia Law Review* 18: 71–123.

Radstone, Susannah. 2008. "Memory Studies: For and Against". *Memory Studies* 1/1: 31–39.

Rawtaer, Iris, Rathi Mahendran, Junhong Yu, Johnson Fam, Lei Feng and Ee Heok Kua. 2015. "Psychosocial Interventions with Art, Music, Tai Chi and Mindfulness for Subsyndromal Depression and Anxiety in Older Adults: A Naturalistic Study in Singapore". *Asia-Pacific Psychiatry* 7/3: 240–50.

Reese, Elaine, and Kate Farrant. 2003. "Social Origins of Reminiscing". In *Autobiographical Memory and the Construction of the Narrative Self*, edited by Robyn Fivush and Catherine A. Haden, 29–48. Mahwah: Erlbaum.

Reese, Elaine, and Robyn Fivush. 2008. "The Development of Collective Remembering". *Memory* 16/3: 201–212.

Rentfrow, Peter J., and Samuel D. Gosling. 2003. "The Do Re Mi's of Everyday Life: The Structure and Personality Correlates of Music Preferences". *Journal of Personality and Social Psychology* 84/6: 1236–256.

—2006. "Message in a Ballad: The Role of Music Preferences in Interpersonal Perception". *Psychological Science* 17/3: 236–42.

Reynolds, Simon. 2011. *Retromania: Pop Culture's Addiction to its Own Past*. London: Faber and Faber.

Robinson, John A. 1992. "First Experience Memories: Contexts and Functions in Personal Histories". In *Theoretical Perspectives on Autobiographical Memory*, edited by Martin A. Conway, David C. Rubin, Hans Spinnler and Willem A. Wagenaar, 223–39. Dordrecht: Kluwer Academic Press.

Rock, Adrienne M. L., Laurel J. Trainor and Tami L. Addison. 1999. "Distinctive Messages in Infant-directed Lullabies and Play Songs". *Developmental Psychology* 35/2: 527–34.

Rosenbaum, Jill and Lorraine Prinsky. 1987. "Sex, Violence and Rock 'n' Roll: Youths' Perceptions of Popular Music". *Popular Music and Society* 11/2: 79–89.

Ross, Bruce M. 1992. *Remembering the Personal Past: Descriptions of Autobiographical Memory*. New York: Oxford University Press.

Rubin, David C. 2000. "The Distribution of Early Childhood Memories". *Memory* 8/4: 265–69.

Rubin, David C., and Dorthe Berntsen. 2009. "The Frequency of Voluntary and Involuntary Autobiographical Memories across the Lifespan". *Memory & Cognition* 37/5: 679–88.

Rubin, David C., and Marc Kozin. 1984. "Vivid Memories". *Cognition* 16/1: 81–95.

Saarikallio, Suvi, and Jaakko Erkkilä. 2007. "The Role of Music in Adolescents' Mood Regulation". *Psychology of Music* 35/1: 88–109.

Sachs, Matthew E., Antonio Damasio and Assal Habibi. 2015. "The Pleasures of Sad Music: A Systematic Review". *Frontiers in Human Neuroscience* 9: 404. https://www.frontiersin.org/articles/10.3389/fnhum.2015.00404/full (accessed 17 December 2018).

Sakamoto, Mayumi, Hiroshi Ando and Akimitsu Tsutou. 2013. "Comparing the Effects of Different Individualized Music Interventions for Elderly Individuals with Severe Dementia". *International Psychogeriatrics* 25/5: 775–84.

Schacter, Daniel L. 2001. *How the Mind Forgets and Remembers: The Seven Sins of Memory*. Boston and New York: Houghton Mifflin.

Schank, Roger C., and Robert P. Abelson. 1995. "Knowledge and Memory: The Real Story". In *Knowledge and Memory: The Real Story*. Advances in Social Cognition, VIII, edited by Robert S. Wyer, Jr., 1–86. Hillsdale: Lawrence Erlbaum Associates Inc.

Scherer, Klaus R., Marcel R. Zentner and Annekathrin Schacht. 2001. "Emotional States Generated by Music: An Exploratory Study of Music Experts". *Musicae Scientiae* 5/1: 149–71.

Schulkind, Matthew D., Laura Kate Hennis and David C. Rubin. 1999. "Music, Emotion and Autobiographical Memory: They're Playing Your Song". *Memory & Cognition* 27/6: 948–55.

Shansky, Carol L. 2014. "Patriotism and the Skirl of the Pipes: The Scottish Highland Pipe Band and World War I British Recruiting in New York, 1916–18". *Journal of Musicological Research* 33/1-3: 241–67.

Shibazaki, Kagari, and Nigel A. Marshall. 2017. "Exploring the Impact of Music Concerts in Promoting Well-being in Dementia Care". *Aging & Mental Health* 21/5: 468–76.

Shum, Michael S. 1998. "The Role of Temporal Landmarks in Autobiographical Memory Processes". *Psychological Bulletin* 124/3: 423–442.

Sixsmith, Judith. 1986. "The Meaning of Home: An Exploratory Study of Environmental Experience". *Journal of Environmental Psychology* 6/4: 281–98.

Skowronski, John J., and W. Richard Walker. 2004. "How Describing Autobiographical Events Can Affect Autobiographical Memory". *Social Cognition* 22/5: 555–90.

Sloboda, John. 2005. *Exploring the Musical Mind: Cognition, Emotion, Ability, Function*. Oxford: Oxford University Press.

—1991. "Music Structure and Emotional Response: Some Empirical Findings". *Psychology of Music* 19/2: 110–20.

Smith, Wyverne. 2008. "Learning a Music Instrument in Early Childhood: What Can We Learn from Professional Musicians' Childhood Memories?" *Australian Journal of Early Childhood* 33/4: 54–62.

Spence, Donald. P. 1988. "Passive Remembering". In *Remembering Reconsidered: Ecological and Traditional Approaches to the Study of Memory*, edited by Ulrich Neisser and Eugene Winograd, 311–25. Cambridge: Cambridge University Press.

Stebbins, Robert A. 1992. *Amateurs, Professionals, and Serious Leisure*. Montreal and Kingston: McGill-Queen's University.

Stengs, Irene. 2018. "Popular Music and Commemorative Ritual: A Material Approach". In *Routledge Companion to Popular Music History and Heritage*, edited by Sarah Baker, Catherine Strong, Lauren Istvandity and Zelmarie Cantillon, 229–37. London and New York: Routledge.

Stewart, Nick Alan Joseph, and Adam Jonathan Lonsdale. 2016. "It's Better Together: The Psychological Benefits of Singing in a Choir". *Psychology of Music* 44/6: 1240–254.

Strachan, Robert. 2007. "Micro-independent Record Labels in the UK: Discourse, DIY Cultural Production and the Music Industry". *European Journal of Cultural Studies* 10/2: 245–65.

Strong, Catherine. 2011. *Grunge: Music and Memory*. Farnham: Ashgate.

Tarrant, Mark, Adrian C. North and David J. Hargreaves. 2002. "Youth Identity and Music". In *Musical Identities*, edited by Raymond Macdonald, David Hargreaves and Dorothy Miell, 134–50. Oxford: Oxford University Press.

ter Bogt, Tom F. M., Marc J. M. H. Delsing, Maarten van Zalk, Peter G. Christenson and Wim H. J. Meeus. 2011. "Intergenerational Continuity of Taste: Parental and Adolescent Music Preferences". *Social Forces* 90/1: 297–319.

Thompson, William Forde. 2015. *Music, Thought, and Feeling: Understanding the Psychology of Music*. Oxford and New York: Oxford University Press.

Turner, Bryan S., and June Edmunds. 2002. "The Distaste of Taste: Bourdieu, Cultural Capital and the Australian Postwar Elite". *Journal of Consumer Culture* 2/2: 219–39.

Unruh, David R. 1983. "Death and Personal History: Strategies of Identity Preservation". *Social Problems* 30/3: 340–51.

Van Dijck, Jose. 2006. "Record and Hold: Popular Music between Personal and Collective Memory". *Critical Studies in Media Communication* 23/5: 357–74.

Van der Hoeven, Arno. 2014. "Remembering the Popular Music of the 1990s: Dance Music and the Cultural Meanings of Decade-based Nostalgia". *International Journal of Heritage Studies* 20/3: 316–30.

Van den Tol, Annemieke J. M., and Jane Edwards. 2013. "Exploring a Rationale for Choosing to Listen to Sad Music When Feeling Sad". *Psychology of Music* 41/4: 440–65.

—2015. "Listening to Sad Music in Adverse Situations: How Music Selection Strategies Relate to Self-regulatory Goals, Listening Effects, and Mood Enhancement". *Psychology of Music* 43/4: 473–94.

Van Zijl, Anemone G. W., and John Sloboda. 2010. "Performers' Experienced Emotions in the Construction of Expressive Musical Performance: An Exploratory Investigation". *Psychology of Music* 39/2: 196–219.

Vroomen, Laura. 2004. "Kate Bush: Teen Pop and Older Female Fans". In *Music Scenes: Local, Translocal, and Virtual*, edited by Andy Bennett and Richard A. Peterson, 238–53. Nashville: Vanderbilt University Press.

Walsh, Michael J. 2010. "Driving to the Beat of One's Own Hum: Automobility and Musical Listening". In *Studies in Symbolic Interaction*, edited by Norman K. Denzin, 201–221. Bingley: Emerald Group.

Walter, Tony. 1996. "A New Model of Grief: Bereavement and Biography". *Mortality* 1/1: 7–25.

Wang, Qi, and Martin A. Conway. 2004. "The Stories We Keep: Autobiographical Memory in American and Chinese Middle-aged Adults". *Journal of Personality* 72/5: 911–38.

Waugh, Earle H. 2005. *Memory, Music, and Religion*. Columbia: University of South Carolina Press.

Whiteley, Sheila. 2000. *Women and Popular Music: Sexuality, Identity and Subjectivity*. London and New York: Routledge.

Whiteley, Sheila, ed. 1997. *Sexing the Groove: Popular Music and Gender*. London and New York: Routledge.

Wilhelm, Kay, Inika Gillis, Emery Schubert and Erin Louise Whittle. 2013. "On a Blue Note: Depressed Peoples' Reasons for Listening to Music". *Music and Medicine* 5/2: 76–83.

Williams, Helen L., Martin A. Conway and Gillian Cohen. 2008. "Autobiographical Memory". In *Memory in the Real World*, edited by Gillian Cohen and Martin A. Conway, 21–90. Sussex; New York: Psychology Press.

Woody, Robert H. 2002. "Emotion, Imagery and Metaphor in the Acquisition of Musical Performance Skill". *Music Education Research* 4/2: 213–24.

Woody, Robert H., and Gary E. McPherson. 2010. "Emotion and Motivation in the Lives of Performers". In *Handbook of Music and Emotion: Theory, Research, Applications*, edited by Patrik N. Juslin and John Sloboda, 401–424. Oxford: Oxford University Press.

Index